Contents

Chapter 1

The Rage Within Us

What do Cain, Moses, King David, the Prophet Jonah and Jesus Christ all have in common? According to the Scriptures, they all experienced anger. Cain became angry with his brother and murdered him. In anger, Moses broke the two tablets of the Law when he came down from the mountain. David became angry and passed judgment, bringing judgment upon himself and his family for years to come.

Anger is a fact of life. Everyone experiences this emotion from time to time. Many righteous people in the Bible became angry—including our Lord Himself. For this reason, God's Word has much to say about the subject of anger—what it is and what it can do. When anger is controlled and is displayed according to biblical principles, it can be a positive force that will bring glory to God. Therefore, it's important that we understand this force and learn to use it in the way God intended.

In this study, we will be examining anger from a biblical perspective, discovering when anger is acceptable to God and learning principles for controlling it. In studying the many forms of anger, we will be looking at key people in the Scriptures who became angry. As we see how these people handled their anger, we in turn will learn the right—and wrong—ways for dealing with the rage within us.

Definition of Anger

What is anger? The dictionary tells us that anger is a strong feeling of displeasure aroused by a real or a supposed wrong. This is an apt definition. We have all experienced this strong feeling of displeasure on many occasions. Perhaps someone has almost sideswiped your car on the highway, forcing you off the road. You are furious with the other driver. Why? Because he had no right to drive in this way. Or you turn on the news and hear about someone who has been abused by another person. You become indignant because something is not being done about this problem. Our anger can be aroused in an instant by any real or imagined wrong committed against ourselves or others.

Anger is a very strong emotion. When it is allowed to continue unchecked, it can destroy the enraged person and others. However, people who deny that they are angry can also be severely hurt. Studies have shown that anger has definite effects on the body. In fact, many doctors are now telling us that suppressed anger can contribute to a number of physical problems and illnesses.

In itself, anger is not evil. God has instilled in us certain emotions—including anger. When these emotions are working together properly, they serve to preserve and to build us. Anger is like a fire. When used correctly, a fire warms and helps us. However, if left to itself, a small fire will soon become a raging inferno, destroying everything in its path. Likewise, anger fuels our emotional defense system when it is used as God has directed.

We are created in the image of God—a God who becomes angry at times. However, the anger displayed by our Lord is always righteous. This, then, is the key to using and controlling anger. The philosopher Aristotle wrote: "Anybody can become angry. That is easy. But to be angry with the right person and to the right degree and at the right time and for the right purpose and in the right way—that is not within everybody's power and is not easy."

Unfortunately, Aristotle was right. Few people have learned how to express this God-given emotion in the way that He intended. All too often we allow our anger to lead to sin. When we mix anger with pride, pettiness, envy or greed, we create serious problems for ourselves and for others. In the lives of David, Cain, Jonah and others in the Bible, we find many vivid illustrations of the destructiveness of sinful anger. However, it is possible to be angry and yet not sin. In Ephesians 4:26 the Apostle Paul said, "Be ye angry, and sin not" (see also Ps. 4:4). The Lord Jesus Christ and Moses both became angry without sinning. When we follow their example in using anger properly and righteously, then anger will become a constructive, rather than destructive, force in our lives.

Distinctions Between Kinds of Anger

Is there more than one kind of anger? Yes. The Bible makes a number of distinctions between types of anger. For instance, in Colossians 3, Paul reminded the believers that since they had been raised with the Lord Jesus Christ, they should concentrate on heavenly matters and should abandon certain life-styles and practices: "But now ye also put off all these; anger, wrath, malice, blasphemy, filthy communication out of your mouth" (v. 8).

Notice that both anger and wrath are listed in this passage. You may be asking yourself, *But aren't these the same?* No. In the Greek text, the words translated "anger" and "wrath" in this verse are different. The Greek word for anger (*orgē*) describes a more settled and lasting kind of inward feeling. It is the type of anger that grows slowly and that often leads to revenge. On the other hand, the Greek word translated "wrath" (*thumos*) indicates a sudden and agitated outburst of anger. It sometimes reflects the ongoing anger that has been smoldering inside. It usually flares up suddenly and then quickly subsides. The Bible has much to say about both of these kinds of anger.

In addition, the Scriptures make a distinction between holy and unholy anger. Many Christians would have a hard time believing that any kind of anger could be holy. They consider all anger to be evil. However, keep in mind that God Himself experiences anger. The Bible is filled with references to the wrath of God. Since the Lord is holy, just and good, He could only express a holy and just anger. Therefore, feeling the emotion of anger is not wrong. Anger can be good and holy when expressed in the same way that the Lord reveals His anger.

What constitutes holy anger? First, it is anger toward sin. God hates sin. If you read the passages that refer to the wrath of God, you will discover that, in each case, He was displaying anger toward sin. When Jesus lashed out at the money changers in the temple, He did so because they were cheating the people and were using God's house for personal gain (see Matt. 21:12,13). God wants us to hate sin. We should be angry at the injustice in the world. Psalm 97:10 tells us, "Ye that love the Lord, hate evil: he preserveth the souls of his saints." If we truly love the Lord, we will become angry whenever we see sins committed against Him or against His children.

Second, holy anger is anger that is controlled by God. This kind of anger shows inner strength and self-restraint. Thomas Fuller, a famous Puritan preacher, once described anger as one of the sinews of the soul. Anger that is controlled by God and directed toward His cause will make you a stronger—not weaker—person.

Third, holy anger is concerned with defending and building up others rather than protecting its own pride and self-esteem. It becomes angry *for* people—not *at* people. It is used as a tool for construction rather than a weapon for destruction. Holy anger is always mixed with a loving concern

9

for people—including the ones who have hurt you or others.

Finally, holy anger produces righteousness rather than sinfulness. It should build up our Christian life—not tear it down. When we are harboring unholy anger, it begins to affect every area of our lives. Our prayer life begins to suffer. We find it hard to pray; and when we do pray, we are unable to do it properly. That's why I Timothy 2:8 instructs us to "pray every where, lifting up holy hands, without wrath and doubting." Holy anger, on the other hand, compels us to share the problem with God in prayer.

Another area that will suffer when we feel unholy anger is our Christian service. This is why James 1:19,20 warns us, "Wherefore, my beloved brethren, let every man be swift to hear, slow to speak, slow to wrath: for the wrath of man worketh not the righteousness of God." When we are nursing hurts and selfish anger, we will not be useful to God in accomplishing His will. However, holy anger fans the flames within us and spurs us into action in defending the grace of God.

Directions for Controlling Anger

The ability to feel anger is a gift from God. The Lord built anger into our emotional system for our benefit. But, as we have seen, not all anger is good. It depends on how we use it. Anger is extremely powerful. Unless it is kept under control, it can be deadly. When anger is allowed to go anywhere it wants to go, it becomes like a river that has overflowed its banks. The normally quiet and peaceful river becomes a raging flood that destroys everything in its path. Thus, learning to control our anger is vital if we are to use it for God's glory and our good.

How can we learn to control our anger? God's Word gives us some specific directions to help us. First, *we must yield to the Holy Spirit.* When we do, He will guide us and produce His fruit in our lives: "The fruit of the Spirit is love, joy, peace, longsuffering, kindness, goodness, faithfulness, gentleness, self-control" (Gal. 5:22,23, NKJV). The Holy Spirit will not only give us the kind of attitudes that ward off anger, but He will also teach us self-control so that we can keep our anger in check when it arises.

Some people have the mistaken idea that when the Holy Spirit takes control of your life, you have no responsibility for self-control. I have participated in Bible conferences with preachers who did not know how to watch the clock. Consequently, when it was my turn to preach, they had used up 15 or 20 minutes of my time. What was their excuse? "Well, Brother Wiersbe," they would say, "you know that when the Spirit takes over, you've just got to keep going." However, the Bible teaches me that when the Spirit of God takes over, we gain more self-control—not less. I've noticed in my own life that when the Holy Spirit is in control, I am able to control my words and my time better, completing tasks when and how they need to be done. In instructing the Corinthian Christians regarding the proper use of spiritual gifts, Paul wrote: "The spirits

11

of the prophets are subject to the prophets. For God is not the author of confusion, but of peace" (I Cor. 14:32,33). If anger or other aspects of our lives are out of control, then God is not the source.

The Holy Spirit can fill us with love, joy, peace, patience, self-control—all we need to keep our anger in check and directed toward useful ends. Anger, wrath, envy and strife are all works of the flesh (see vv. 19-21). But when our anger is under the Spirit's control, then we are able to use it as a tool for building rather than as a weapon for destruction.

In order to control our anger, we not only need the fullness of the Holy Spirit but also *we must be humble and honest.* In the Sermon on the Mount, Jesus warned us of the dangerous consequences of anger: "Ye have heard that it was said by them of old time, Thou shalt not kill; and whosoever shall kill shall be in danger of the judgment: but I say unto you, That whosoever is angry with his brother without a cause shall be in danger of the judgment" (Matt. 5:21,22). The Lord then gave us further instructions for dealing with our anger: "Therefore if thou bring thy gift to the altar, and there rememberest that thy brother hath ought against thee; leave there thy gift before the altar, and go thy way; first be reconciled to thy brother, and then come and offer thy gift" (vv. 23,24).

So often our anger is unwarranted. We become enraged over some imagined wrong. Christ's words speak to us of the importance of evaluating our angry feelings to see if they are really justified. We need to pray, asking the Lord if we said or did something that we should not have said or done. And if we are at fault, we need to take steps to rectify the problem. We must honestly and humbly go to the person with whom we are angry and seek his forgiveness. This is not easy to do. It is even more difficult to go to someone who has genuinely wronged us and take the first steps toward reconciliation. Our pride tells us, "I'm not going to apologize to him. It was his fault, and he should come to me!" However, if we truly want to gain control over our anger, we must develop the kind of humility and honesty that not only admits when we are wrong but also goes the extra mile in seeking peace. Without it, our relationship with the Lord will suffer and the Body of Christ will be torn apart.

Third, in order to control our anger, *we need to use our tongue carefully.* In Proverbs 15:1 we are told, "A soft answer turneth away wrath: but grievous words stir up anger." Conversations are like small fires. The more fuel you add to them, the more they blaze. Nothing cools a person's temper faster than a calm, quiet response. We need to remember that it takes two people to have an argument. Many angry arguments and hurt feelings could be avoided if people would learn to control their tongues. If we are allowing the Holy Spirit to control us, He will give us the strength we need to give a soft answer to the person who lashes out at us with angry words.

Fourth, *we need to remember the consequences of anger.* Looking ahead and realizing what will happen if we become angry is one of the best deterrents to uncontrolled anger. Proverbs 19:19 states, "A man of great wrath shall suffer punishment: for if thou deliver him, yet thou must do it again." In other words, the person who has an uncontrollable temper, who flares up at the slightest provocation, will constantly create trouble for himself and for others. Angry people say and do things they later regret. However, even though they repent and are truly sorry for the trouble they have caused, they can never undo the damage. The physical and emotional scars they have inflicted will always remain.

Not only do we need to think about the results of our anger, but also *we must develop a proper perspective toward anger.* In Proverbs 19:11, we discover what our perspective should be: "The discretion of a man defereth his anger; and it is his glory to pass over a transgression." We need to use discretion and prudence in determining when to become angry. Anger drains us physically, mentally and emotionally. And many so-called injustices are so trivial that they simply don't deserve the huge investment of our time and energy that anger demands. Proverbs 14:29 tells us, "He that is slow to wrath is of great understanding: but he that is hasty of spirit exalteth folly." Uncontrolled anger can hurt us even more than it hurts the other person. That's why it is so important to have a proper perspective toward the things that happen to us. One of the best qualities for controlling anger is a sense of humor. We need to learn to laugh off people's unintentional, rude actions and thoughtless words. Rather than harboring anger and resentment, we need to tell ourselves, "Oh, he didn't mean that" or "Well, she probably didn't realize she was bothering me." When we see these hurts in the proper light, we won't waste our precious energy nursing needless grudges.

In order to have a proper perspective toward anger, *we must develop Christian character.* The more we become like Christ, the stronger we will be. And, as Proverbs 16:32 tells us, it takes more strength to subdue our anger than to defeat an entire army: "He that is slow to anger is better than the mighty; and he that ruleth his spirit than he that taketh a city." We have an army that is waging war within us. If we allow the army to revolt, our anger will take over and we will do things we shouldn't do. When we cultivate Christian character, we will learn to forgive as Christ forgives. We will leave our anger at the cross. In Ephesians 4:32, Paul wrote: "Be ye kind one to another, tenderhearted, forgiving one another, even as God for Christ's sake hath forgiven you." If someone does something that hurts you and you want to respond in anger, just go to the cross and remember how much God has forgiven you.

Finally, *we need to remember that God is the judge.* Romans 12:19 tells us, "Dearly beloved, avenge not yourselves, but rather give place unto wrath: for it is written, Vengeance is mine; I will repay, saith the Lord." Only God has the ability to judge fairly. He is not only aware of our actions, but He also knows the thoughts and intentions behind them. We can easily be deceived by a person's appearance and actions. Someone who may appear to be our friend could really be our enemy and vice versa. Therefore, we need to leave judgment and retribution to God. Our job is to love those who hurt us: "If thine enemy hunger, feed him; if he thirst, give him drink. . . . Be not overcome of evil, but overcome evil with good" (vv. 20,21). This is where faith enters in. When people cause us to be angry and hurt, we must be willing to give the problem to God and trust Him to take care of it.

Anger is a wonderful gift from God. When this emotion is displayed according to God's directives, it can be a positive force in our lives. However, anger can also be terribly destructive if it is not controlled. May God give us the grace to control the rage within us and to use it for His glory.

Chapter 2

Cain: Anger Closes the Doors

As we have seen, anger can be good when it is used for the glory of God and controlled according to the principles given in the Scriptures. However, uncontrolled and selfish anger destroys ourselves and others. Instead of glorifying God, this kind of anger leads us away from Him. Probably no other person in the Bible illustrates this sad fact more than Cain. His anger led to other sins—including murder. What caused his anger? What were the results? Do these same truths apply to us today?

Cain's problem with anger teaches us that sin is not merely one act—it is a process. And it's a process that leads to death. James 1:13-15 describes this process in terms of pregnancy and birth: "Let no man say when he is tempted, I am tempted of God: for God cannot be tempted with evil, neither tempteth he any man: but every man is tempted, when he is drawn away of his own lust, and enticed. Then when lust hath conceived, it bringeth forth sin: and sin, when it is finished [full grown], bringeth forth death."

Anger was not Cain's only problem. It was just one of several steps that eventually led him away

17

from God and into sin and isolation. By understanding what happened to Cain, we can guard against making the same mistakes in our own lives.

Unbelief

The first step in Cain's downfall was *unbelief*. Genesis 4:3-5 tells us, "And in process of time it came to pass, that Cain brought of the fruit of the ground an offering unto the Lord. And Abel, he also brought of the firstlings of his flock and of the fat thereof. And the Lord had respect unto Abel and to his offering: but unto Cain and to his offering he had not respect." Why did God not honor Cain's offering? Because it was not brought in faith. The Lord had given them specific instructions for sacrificing to Him, and Cain willfully chose to disobey God's directives.

What were God's instructions for worship? From the beginning, He taught man that a sacrifice of blood was needed to atone for sin. The Lord even set the example by clothing Adam and Eve in animal skins after the Fall. When the time came for Cain and Abel to bring their own offerings, Abel came to the altar by faith, sacrificing the best of his lambs as God had prescribed. Thus, his offering was accepted by God. As a result, Abel has earned a place among the people of faith: "By faith Abel offered unto God a more excellent sacrifice than Cain, by which he obtained witness that he was righteous, God testifying of his gifts: and by it he being dead yet speaketh" (Heb. 11:4).

Cain, on the other hand, ignored God's instructions and tried to worship in his own way. When we follow his example, we are said to be following the "way of Cain" (Jude 1:11). What is the way of Cain? It's the way of unbelief—of bringing God good works instead of faith. Cain sacrificed simply because this is what he had been told to do. His heart had not been changed. Any act of worship is worthless if our heart is not in it. God looks first at the worshiper, then at the sacrifice.

In the Book of Isaiah, we find God condemning the people of Israel for bringing sacrifices when their hearts were not in their offerings: "To what purpose is the multitude of your sacrifices unto me? saith the Lord: I am full of the burnt-offerings of rams, and the fat of fed beasts; and I delight not in the blood of bullocks, or of lambs, or of he goats. When ye come to appear before me, who hath required this at your hand, to tread my courts? Bring no more vain oblations; incense is an abomination unto me; the new moons and sabbaths, the calling of assemblies, I cannot away with; it is iniquity, even the solemn meeting" (1:11-13). The Lord then told the people what they must do before He would again accept their sacrifices: "Wash you, make you clean; put away the evil of your doings from before mine eyes; cease to do evil" (v. 16). God cannot tolerate sin and disobedience. Therefore, He could not accept the people's worship until their hearts were right with Him.

God rejected Cain's sacrifice because his attitude was wrong. Cain's heart was not with God. In I John 3:12, we discover that Cain had a problem with sin

19

long before he killed Abel: "Not as Cain, who was of that wicked one, and slew his brother. And wherefore slew he him? Because his own works were evil, and his brother's righteous." God not only rejected Cain's offering; He considered it to be evil. Why? Because Cain's heart was evil. He did not have faith. And unbelief is at the heart of all other sins.

Anger

Cain's unbelief soon led to jealousy and anger: "But unto Cain and to his offering he had not respect. And Cain was very wroth [angry], and his countenance fell" (Gen. 4:5). Notice where Cain became angry—at the altar. We can be overcome with anger at any place and any time—even during a worship service in God's house. Therefore, we must always be ready to ward off these attacks of Satan.

Why was Cain's anger sinful? Because *he was angry at the wrong persons.* He was angry at God for not accepting him and his sacrifice. And he was angry at Abel because he had been accepted. In both cases his anger was unjustified. Rather than being angry at them, Cain should have been angry with himself for disobeying God.

Cain's anger was also sinful because *he was angry for the wrong reasons.* God had given Cain specific directions for worship. All he had to do to be accepted was to follow the Lord's instructions. But Cain wanted to be accepted on his own terms. He willfully disobeyed and then became angry when God rejected his sacrifice. But the Lord told him,

"Why art thou wroth [angry]? and why is thy countenance fallen? If thou doest well, shalt thou not be accepted?" (vv. 6,7). In other words, God was saying to him, "Why are you angry? Didn't I tell you how to do it? I'm not going to change my standards just for you."

When we become angry at God, often it is because He has not answered our prayers in the way we think He should. Or many times we have committed some sin and are using anger to cover up our feelings of guilt. Both of these are the wrong reasons for feeling angry.

Likewise, *Cain's anger toward Abel had the wrong basis.* At its roots were feelings of jealousy and pride rather than indignation at being genuinely wronged. He was envious of his brother's righteousness and favor in God's eyes (see I John 3:12). Abel's obedience also reminded Cain of his own guilt. Instead of expressing anger and remorse for his sin, Cain vented his feelings on Abel.

Temptation

When Cain closed the door on God through unbelief, he left the door wide open for Satan to enter. God warned Cain about the possible consequences of his disobedience: "If thou doest well, shalt thou not be accepted? and if thou doest not well, sin lieth at the door. And unto thee shall be his desire, and thou shalt rule over him" (Gen. 4:7). In the Hebrew language, the word translated "lieth" pictures sin as a lion crouching at the door. In other words, God was telling Cain, "Beware, Cain, for temptation is right outside the door. If you are not careful, it will pounce on you, and you will be devoured by sin."

Temptation is like a crouching lion—it simply waits for the right opportunity to seize us. The Apostle Peter warned us of the danger awaiting us: "Be sober, be vigilant; because your adversary the devil, as a roaring lion, walketh about, seeking whom he may devour" (I Pet. 5:8). When Cain opened the door to anger, he gave the Devil a foothold in his heart. He left the door open just wide enough for temptation to enter. Cain gave Satan free rein over his anger, and the Devil used it to lead him into other sins.

Cain could have avoided many problems if he had simply been honest with himself and with God. When the Lord asked him, "Why are you angry?" Cain should have admitted that he was wrong for asking God to accept his offering and then should have brought the right sacrifice of faith. However, instead of repenting, he allowed his unbelief and anger to remain and grow in his heart. Because of his unbelief, Cain closed the door on God. Because of his anger, he closed the door on his brother. And, in doing so, he left the door open to Satan.

Whenever we are out of fellowship with God and with our brothers and sisters in Christ, we are vulnerable to the attacks of the Wicked One. This is why misplaced and prolonged anger is so danger-ous. Anger leads to sin when we allow it to remain. For this reason, we need to heed the warning of Ephesians 4:25-27: "Wherefore putting away lying, speak every man truth with his neighbour: for we are members one of another. Be ye angry, and sin not: let not the sun go down upon your wrath: neither give place to the devil."

Murder

The combination of unbelief and temptation almost always produces sin. In Cain's case, his unbelief and anger led to deadly results—murder. "And Cain talked with Abel his brother: and it came to pass, when they were in the field, that Cain rose up against Abel his brother, and slew him" (Gen. 4:8).

We don't know what Cain and Abel were talking about. Cain possibly used some ploy, such as wanting to show him something, to lure Abel out to the field. Whatever he said, it was undoubtedly subtle, for Abel appears to have no clue of Cain's intentions. But Cain could not hide the anger in his heart forever. It eventually emerged in a violent way. Cain attacked his brother and viciously killed him.

Many people think that any kind of anger is not sinful so long as we do not express it openly. But Jesus emphatically stated that harboring anger toward someone is the same as murdering that person: "Ye have heard that it was said by them of old time, Thou shalt not kill; and whosoever shall kill shall be in danger of the judgment: but I say unto you, That whosoever is angry with his brother without a cause shall be in danger of the judgment" (Matt. 5:21,22). In other words, our Lord is saying

23

that when we are angry with a person, we are, in effect, murdering him. We don't have to commit the actual act of murder in order to be guilty of it. Why did Jesus condemn anger so strongly? Because He knew that all unholy anger will ultimately result in some outward, sinful expression. We will say or do something to hurt the other person.

God hates murder (see Prov. 6:17). Exodus 20:13 clearly states, "Thou shalt not kill." A more accurate translation of this would be "Thou shalt not murder." In this commandment, God is not talking about accidently killing someone or killing in self-defense. He is referring to the willful and intentional taking of another person's life.

Murder is serious, not only because the killer is taking a life that God has given but also because he is usurping God's authority. God is the giver and sustainer of life. "In him we live, and move, and have our being" (Acts 17:28). As such, He alone has the right to determine when our lives will end. Likewise, He is the great Lawgiver and Judge. God is the only one who has the right to determine how we will die. Cain took it upon himself to become God and, in the process, murdered his own brother out of selfishness, anger, envy and pride.

While our anger may not cause us to commit murder, it is still just as sinful. Hurting anyone in any way—whether by our words or by our actions—is the same as murdering him in God's eyes. Anger that is based on unbelief, envy, pride or other sinful attitudes is always wrong and will lead us into temptation and sin.

Deceit

But the sin process doesn't stop with unbelief, anger, temptation and the outward act of sinning. Once we have sinned, we commit more sins to hide the first one. And the process just keeps on going.

Sin almost always leads to deceit. Cain tried to lie to God in order to hide his sin. But he learned—as we all do—that he could not deceive God. "And the Lord said unto Cain, Where is Abel thy brother? And he said, I know not: Am I my brother's keeper?" (Gen. 4:9). When God asked Cain this question, He didn't do so to gain information. He knew exactly where Abel was and what Cain had done. The Lord was forcing Cain to face himself.

But Cain evaded the issue. Rather than admitting his sin, he made light of it, saying, "Am I my brother's keeper?" (v. 9). When we remember that Abel was a shepherd, this comment takes on added meaning. We can just hear Cain jokingly say, "Am I the keeper's keeper? Am I the shepherd's shepherd? He's a shepherd; he can take care of himself."

When we allow Satan to take control of our lives, as Cain did, then lying will become part of our nature, for the Devil is the master liar. In John 8:44 Jesus said, "Ye are of your father the devil, and the lusts of your father ye will do. He was a murderer from the beginning. . . . When he speaketh a lie, he speaketh of his own: for he is a liar, and the father of it." Like all sin, lying follows a progression. Cain first lied to Abel in order to lure him out into the field. He then lied to himself, saying, "I can kill Abel, and no one will ever have to know." And finally Cain lied to God, saying, "I don't know where Abel is. Am I my brother's keeper?" We find this same sequence of deceit in I John 1. Three times in this chapter we find the phrase "if we say." First we lie to others, then we lie to ourselves, and then we lie to God. The only way to break this dangerous pattern of deceit is by confessing our sin and asking God to help us speak the truth: "If we confess our sins, he is faithful and just to forgive us our sins, and to cleanse us from all unrighteousness" (v. 9). Cain could have avoided much heartache if he would have simply confessed his sin to God rather than trying to hide it from Him.

Despair

Cain thought that he could cover up his sin by lying about it, but he soon discovered that deceit only leads to despair. God was not fooled for one moment by his glibness. The Lord reprimanded Cain severely, saying, "What hast thou done? the voice of thy brother's blood crieth unto me from the ground. And now art thou cursed from the earth" (Gen. 4:10,11).

Because Cain chose to lie about his sin, his punishment was even more severe. The Lord cursed Cain, just as He had cursed the serpent in the Garden (see 3:14). While God had cursed Satan and had cursed the ground because of Adam's sin (see v. 17), this was the first time He had cursed a human being. "And now art thou cursed from the earth, which hath opened her mouth to receive thy brother's blood from thy hand; when thou tillest the ground, it shall not henceforth yield unto thee her strength; a fugitive and a vagabond shalt thou be in the earth" (4:11,12).

Because of his sin, Cain was doomed to live as a wanderer and a fugitive for the rest of his life. No longer could he be a farmer, for the earth would not grow anything he planted. He would spend the rest of his life running from God. Notice Cain's response to God's verdict: "My punishment is greater than I can bear" (v. 13). Even after coming face to face with his sin, Cain still didn't feel remorse or guilt. He was only concerned about his punishment.

Sin comes between us and God, causing our fellowship with Him to be severed. And separation from God brings despair and loneliness. But it does not need to be this way. The Lord is waiting for us to bring our sin and guilt to Him so that we can enjoy the healing power of His forgiveness and love.

Rejection

Sin that is unconfessed eventually leads to despair and rejection. God had opened His arms to Cain. He had told him how to worship. When Cain disobeyed this command, the Lord tried to warn him to come back before he gave in to temptation. Then when Cain sinned, God gave him a chance to confess his sin and receive forgiveness. But Cain rejected God's offers for help. He turned his back on the Lord and tried to make it on his own.

Genesis 4:16 tells us, "And Cain went out from the presence of the Lord, and dwelt in the land of

Nod." The word "Nod" means "wandering." If Cain had repented and had come back to the Lord, he could have been a pilgrim in life, journeying toward his final destination—the city of God (see Heb. 11:10). But because he rejected God, Cain had no home on earth or in heaven. He had no purpose or reason for living. He became a wanderer and a fugitive, forever living on substitutes. He built his own city in an effort to make up for not having a home with God (see Gen. 4:17). Cain put into his city every substitute he could find so he would not need God. And isn't this exactly what our society is doing today? But, like Cain, they are discovering that nothing can replace a relationship with the Lord.

The process of sin starts with unbelief. If we do not have a right relationship with the Lord through faith, we will not relate in the right way to others. We will harbor unhealthy attitudes toward them—including anger. And anger opens the door to Satan and gives him a foothold for temptation. Without a firm foundation of faith, we will not be able to overcome these temptations. We will allow Satan to lead us into all kinds of sin. And sin that is allowed to continue leads to deceit, despair and, ultimately, rejection of God. Thus, the first step in overcoming anger in our lives is to seek a closer relationship with the Lord. We need to confess to Him that anger is a problem in our lives and allow Him to open the doors of forgiveness and healing to us.

The doors are open.

Will we go in by faith?

Chapter 3

Moses: Anger Gives You Courage

If you want to understand a person's character, find out what makes that person laugh, what makes him weep and what makes him angry. Cain's anger was a sign of a sinful, selfish character. Because his anger toward God and toward his brother was misplaced and unjustified, it resulted in temptation and sin.

But not all anger is sinful. Anger can reveal a holy and righteous character—when it is displayed for the right reasons and in the right manner. One of the best examples of righteous anger is found in the life of Moses. Following their miraculous deliverance from Egypt, Moses led the Children of Israel to the foot of Mount Sinai. Moses then journeyed up the mountain to receive God's Law. When he still had not returned after many days, the people became restless and doubtful of his return. They came to Aaron and said, "Up, make us gods, which shall go before us; for as for this Moses, the man that brought us up out of the land of Egypt, we wot [know] not what is become of him" (Ex. 32:1). Aaron agreed to their foolish request. He instructed them to bring their gold jewelry, which he fashioned

29

into the shape of a calf. He then declared a day of feasting, and the people sacrificed to this representation of God (see vv. 2-6).

But the people had forgotten that it was God—not Moses—who had brought them out of Egypt. In making the golden calf, the people were rejecting God. And their sin did not go unnoticed. On the mountain, the Lord told Moses, "My wrath is now going to burn against these people, because they have turned quickly away from My commandment" (see v. 10). Moses pleaded with the Lord to spare the people, and God honored his fervent prayer (see vv. 11-14).

When Moses had finished praying and communing with the Lord, he came down from the mountain. "And it came to pass, as soon as he came nigh unto the camp, that he saw the calf, and the dancing: and Moses' anger waxed hot, and he cast the tables out of his hands, and brake them beneath the mount. And he took the calf which they had made, and burnt it in the fire, and ground it to powder, and strawed [scattered] it upon the water, and made the children of Israel drink of it" (vv. 19,20).

Was Moses justified in his anger? Yes. Here we see him displaying a righteous anger against sin. Even in his actions, he was not merely punishing the people. His actions were object lessons to bring the people back to God. He broke the tablets of the Law to show the people how they had broken God's Law and were not worthy to receive it. He burned the calf and made the people drink it to show them the futility of their idol worship. They had been serving a god who was even weaker than they were.

When Moses had finished rebuking the people, he called for a new and greater commitment to God from them, saying, "Who is on the Lord's side? let him come unto me" (v. 26). He then instructed those who had come to mete out the Lord's punishment on those who had not repented, and 3000 people were slain because of their sin (see vv. 27,28).

As we will see, there are a number of reasons why Moses was justified in his anger. First, he had the right motivation—he was displaying a holy anger against sin. Second, he had a right relationship with God; he had prepared himself for the encounter through prayer and fellowship with the Lord. Third, he displayed his anger in the right manner so that it was constructive rather than destructive. And fourth, he had the right attitude in his anger. His anger was motivated not out of hatred but rather out of love—love for God and for the people. Psalm 119 talks about this righteous kind of anger. The psalmist wrote: "Horror hath taken hold upon me because of the wicked that forsake thy law" (v. 53). When Moses saw how the people were so grievously sinning, he experienced a heartfelt horror and fear for them. Likewise, Moses' anger was not merely a deep resentment or indignation at being wronged; it was a brokenhearted anguish. He grieved for the people, just as the psalmist did: "Rivers of waters run down mine eyes, because they keep not thy law" (v. 136). "I beheld the transgressors, and was grieved; because they kept not thy word" (v. 158). When our anger is motivated out of concern for the sinner and for the integrity of God's Word, it will always be displayed in righteous and useful ways.

Who Sinned

A closer examination of this incident reveals several considerations that show why Moses was justified in his anger. First is the realization of *Who had sinned*. If it had been the Ammonites, Moabites, Perizzites or other Canaanites, we could understand why they had sinned by worshiping an idol. But these were the Children of Israel—God's chosen people.

A pastor was preaching a series of messages on the sins of the saints. One of the church members approached him and said, "I don't like it when you preach about sin in the lives of believers. After all, sin in the life of a Christian is different from sin in the life of an unsaved person." And wisely the pastor responded, "Yes, it's worse."

When we consider everything the Israelites had received from God, it is hard to understand how they could reject Him as they did. First, they had been *chosen by God's grace*. God had called Abraham, promising him, "I will make you a great nation. Your descendants will be as numberless as the sands of the sea. I will make a covenant with them, and they will be My people" (see Gen. 12:1-3). Through the years, God's special blessing and protection had been on these chosen people. Even as they were sinning against God with their idolatry and immorality, they were traveling to the abundant land that God had promised to give them.

Not only did the Israelites have an honored place as God's chosen people, but also they had just been *delivered by God's power* from the land of Egypt (see Ex. 12-14). This incident on Mount Sinai took place only three or four months after they left Egypt. For almost 200 years, the nation of Israel had lived as slaves in Egypt. There they had been surrounded by idolatry. Apparently some of that idolatry had remained in their hearts. For even though they had just been miraculously delivered from bondage, even though they had seen the power of God bring Egypt to its knees, even though they had seen the Red Sea opened to allow them to go through on dry ground, even though they had seen God defeat the enemy who came to attack them, at the first sign of trouble they bowed down before an idol that they themselves had made. No wonder Moses was angry!

The Children of Israel were also a people who were being *fed by God's goodness* each morning. It hadn't taken long for the supplies this vast multitude had taken with them to be depleted. But once again God protected and cared for His children. Each morning they awoke to find the ground covered with manna (see ch. 16). Yet no sooner had the Lord begun to feed them than they were complaining about eating manna every day. So He supplied quail for them as well (see Num. 11). And when they could not find water, He brought water from a rock to meet their needs (see Ex. 17:1-7). God was

33

leading them and feeding them, and what were they doing? They were turning against Him.

If all this wasn't enough to warrant their devotion, the Israelites had also been *included in God's covenant*. In Exodus 19, the Lord made a lasting covenant with the people: "Now therefore, if ye will obey my voice indeed, and keep my covenant, then ye shall be a peculiar [special] treasure unto me above all people: for all the earth is mine: and ye shall be unto me a kingdom of priests, and an holy nation" (vv. 5,6). At the time, the people had responded piously, "All that the Lord hath spoken we will do" (v. 8). After all that God had done for them in keeping His word, we find these same people bowing down before a golden calf just a few months later.

The Children of Israel had been chosen by God's grace, delivered by God's power, fed by God's goodness and graciously included in God's covenant. They had promised to obey Him. They were on their way to God's inheritance. Yet what were they doing? They were practicing idolatry and immorality. They corrupted themselves and turned away from the Lord. When we consider who had sinned, we can see why Moses' anger was justified.

Where They Sinned

If the Children of Israel had only stopped to remember who they were and Whose they were, they would not have made such a foolish request of Aaron. Their sin becomes even more grievous when you consider *where they sinned*. They were at Mount Sinai to receive God's Law, including the law that emphatically stated, "Thou shalt not make unto thee any graven image. . . . Thou shalt not bow down thyself to them, nor serve them" (Ex. 20:4,5).

Not only were they at Mount Sinai to receive the Law, but they were in the presence of God. The Lord had appeared on the mountain as a fire and had spoken to the people directly, giving them His Law (see 19:18—20:21). Later, Moses returned to the mountain to receive further instructions. Throughout the 40 days and nights Moses remained on the mountain, this fire was visible to the Children of Israel (see 24:13-18). In fact, the mountain was still on fire when Moses returned. Deuteronomy 9:15 tells us that Moses had to travel through smoke and fire on his way down. The Children of Israel were in the very presence of God. Yet even as they watched the display of His glory on the mountain, they formed and bowed down to an idol. They were at Mount Sinai to receive God's Law, and yet they were disobeying the Law they had promised to keep.

It seems unbelievable that these people could reject God and His Law only days after they had seen His glory and heard His voice. Yet it shows us vividly how weak man really is and how impossible it is for the Law to save us. Romans 8:3 tells us, "For what the law could not do, in that it was weak through the flesh, God sending his own Son in the likeness of sinful flesh, and for sin, condemned sin in the flesh." Notice that the Law was not weak. The flesh—those trying to obey the Law—was weak.

The Children of Israel affirmed their oath to obey God's Law, not realizing that it's impossible for man to obey the Law of God by relying on human strength. Those who think that they can reach heaven by keeping the Ten Commandments or doing good works need to read the story of the Israelites again. Throughout the Old Testament, we find the Children of Israel sinning repeatedly. They were constantly bowing down to idols and committing immorality in the name of religion. The Law could not change them or control them—it could only condemn them.

Some people would claim that Moses' actions were too harsh, in that he broke both of the tablets when the people had only broken one law. But the writer James clearly tells us, "For whosoever shall keep the whole law, and yet offend in one point, he is guilty of all" (James 2:10). The Law can be compared to a chain with ten links in it. Imagine that you are hanging over a chasm, holding on to this chain. How many links have to break before you will fall? When the Children of Israel broke the one law against idolatry, they were guilty of breaking all of God's Law. And when we consider that these people of God had just received this Law from the Lord Himself, it makes Moses' anger all the more reasonable.

How They Sinned

In understanding the reasons for Moses' anger and the biblical precedent he set in handling it, we need to consider not only who was involved and where they were at the time but also *how they sinned*. God hates all sin, but probably no sin is more personally hateful to Him than idolatry. In worshiping the golden calf, the Israelites were not only rejecting God's Law; they were rejecting the Lord Himself.

The severity of their sin becomes even more apparent as we consider the object of their worship—a golden calf. We don't know exactly what it looked like, but we do know that it was a molten image made out of gold. I also get the impression that it was engraved. It may not have been a huge image, but it was big enough for the people to see and to dance around. They put an altar before it and offered sacrifices to it.

Why did the Israelites make their idol in the image of a calf? Because their neighbors in Egypt and Canaan worshiped a calf. I can imagine all these heathen people watching the Israelites and saying, "These Jews are just like us. They're worshiping a golden calf. Why, these are our people!" Not only did the Children of Israel reject their Father; they lost their testimony. Psalm 106:19-22 tells us how grievous this sin really was: "They made a calf in Horeb, and worshipped the molten image. Thus they changed their glory into the similitude of an ox that eateth grass. They forgat God their saviour, which had done great things in Egypt; wondrous works in the land of Ham, and terrible things by the Red sea." The Children of Israel turned away from the glory of God they had seen on Mount Sinai, exchanging it for an image of one of His creatures.

And men have been doing this ever since (see Rom. 1:21-23).

When Moses saw this grievous sin, he became intensely angry. In his response, we can see the motivation behind his anger. He was angry not so much at the sinners but at the sin. Moses was concerned about God's glory. He could not bear to see His glory marred and His name scorned. Even in begging God to spare the people, Moses was concerned that He would be glorified (see Ex. 32:11-14). He told the Lord, "O God, forgive these people for Your own glory." Do we have this kind of concern for God's glory today? Do we become angry and defend His great name whenever we see people sinning against Him?

Why They Sinned

Considering the Israelites' favored position with God and everything they had seen Him do in recent months, it is especially hard to understand *why they sinned*. But Exodus 32:1 gives us the answer— *unbelief* and *impatience*. The people did not trust the Lord implicitly. At the first sign of trouble, their faith always wavered. Likewise, they were not willing to wait for His will to be revealed. They constantly tried to run ahead of God and do things their own way.

Their lack of faith and their impatience were apparent long before they sinned. In Exodus 19, we discover that the Lord had originally intended to give all the Law to the people directly. But when His voice thundered from the mountain, the people became frightened and told Moses, "We don't want to hear God's voice; we can't stand it. You go speak with the Lord and then come back and tell us what He said" (see 20:19). So Moses spent 40 days on the mountain, meeting with God. During this time the Lord not only gave Him the Ten Commandments and other laws but also gave him detailed instructions for the tabernacle. He told Moses exactly how to build it, what materials to use and how to conduct the sacrifices and other acts of worship there. God instituted tabernacle worship so that the people might maintain a holy walk with Him.

But while Moses was on the mountain working for the people, praying for them and learning for them, what were they doing? They were growing impatient. Unbelief usually leads to impatience. If we are trusting the Lord, we will be willing to wait patiently for Him to lead as He chooses. Isaiah 28:16 tells us, "He that believeth shall not make haste."

Not only were the Children of Israel impatient but *ungrateful* as well. When Moses didn't return right away, they replaced him with Aaron. Everything that Moses had taught them and done for them was quickly swept aside in their desire to have their own way. Moses had left Aaron in charge while he was gone (see Ex. 24:14). But Aaron proved to be a weak leader who bent to the wishes of the majority. When they asked him to build them an idol, he quickly complied, even though he knew it was wrong. Later, when Moses confronted Aaron with his sin, he made excuses and blamed it on the people and even on the furnace, saying, "Thou

39

knowest the people, that they are set on mischief. For they said unto me, Make us gods. . . . So they gave it me: then I cast it into the fire, and there came out this calf" (32:22-24).

Moses became angry at the people because he realized that their sin was a sin of unbelief and rebellion against God. They had replaced Moses with Aaron, they had replaced God with a golden calf, and they had replaced holy living with idolatrous, immoral worship. Idolatry and immorality always go together. Behind the people's wish for the golden calf was their secret desire to go back to Egypt. They didn't believe God when He promised to give them a great land as an inheritance. They looked at the desert around them and longed to go back to the security they had known in Egypt— forgetting completely about the suffering and slavery they had also experienced there. So they rebelled against God and against the leadership of Moses. Acts 7:39-41 tells us, "Whom our fathers would not obey, but thrust him from them, and their hearts turned back again into Egypt, saying unto Aaron, Make us gods to go before us: for as for this Moses, which brought us out of the land of Egypt, we wot [know] not what is become of him. And they made a calf in those days, and offered sacrifice unto the idol, and rejoiced in the works of their own hands." Notice especially the phrase "their hearts turned back again into Egypt" (v. 39). While the Israelites had been taken out of Egypt, Egypt had not been taken out of them. They were still looking back instead of looking up.

Exodus 32:6 tells us that the people rose early in the morning to have this idolatrous feast. It's amazing how people who are too tired to get up early for prayer or Bible study can rise at the crack of dawn for some sinful activity. Likewise, the Israelites gladly contributed their gold to build this idol. It's amazing what people are willing to pay for entertainment and sin, while begrudging what little they give for the Lord's work.

In Exodus 32 we see three philosophies of life. Some, like the Israelites, believe in doing only what is easy and enjoyable. They live by the motto "If it feels good, do it." Then there are those, like Aaron, who do what is popular. They believe that morality is based solely on what is accepted by the majority of society at that time. And finally we have the faithful few, like Moses, who do what is right—no matter what the cost. Their lives are not based on outward circumstances or on the opinions of others but solely on the Word of Truth.

We need more leaders like Moses today. Moses was not concerned about his own pleasure or popularity; he cared only about the glory of the Lord. He was a man of *courage.* He confronted an entire nation with their sin. He told his own brother, "You've sinned." And yet he was also a great man of *compassion.* He went back up on the mountain and begged the Lord to forgive the people; and if He couldn't, then Moses wanted to be punished along with the people (see v. 32). The Apostle Paul also had this kind of compassion. He wrote: "I have great heaviness and continual sorrow in my heart.

41

For I could wish that myself were accursed from Christ for my brethren" (Rom. 9:2,3). Paul was willing to forfeit his own salvation in order to see others come to know the Lord. And, of course, our Lord Jesus took the punishment for our sins. He became a curse for our sakes (see Gal. 3:13). As His followers, we are called to have this same kind of courage and compassion.

When we consider the sin of the Israelites, we can see that Moses' anger was indeed justified and was within the will of God. Unfortunately, few Christians today display this kind of holy anger. We have become so tolerant of sin that we no longer weep or become frightened when we see what people are doing. My prayer is that God will help us, like Moses, to have a holy anger that comes from a broken heart that is willing to make any sacrifice to bring glory to God.

Chapter 4

David: Angry at Other People's Sins

How often do you become angry at other people's sins? Somehow it is always easier to find fault with others than with ourselves. While it is good to be angry at the sins of others if our anger is justified, we must hate our own sins above all and should seek God's cleansing forgiveness for them. Otherwise, we will be brought to our knees in repentance in much more drastic ways.

In II Samuel 12, we find King David making this mistake. Instead of feeling anger and remorse for his own sin, he became angry at the sin of another. As a result, the Lord, through the Prophet Nathan, had to deal with David in order to bring him to the place of repentance.

When we think of King David, a number of different images come to mind. We think of David the shepherd, faithfully caring for his father's sheep. And when the experienced Israelite soldiers were afraid to go against Goliath, this shepherd boy stepped out in faith and defeated the giant (see I Sam. 17:37-51). Or we remember David the soldier. How courageously David went out to fight the battles of the Lord! Likewise, we think of David the singer. He has left us with a wealth of beautiful songs in the Psalms.

Unfortunately, when we think of this man, we can't help but remember David the sinner. He committed adultery by taking Uriah's wife, Bathsheba. David then had his loyal soldier, Uriah, murdered in an effort to cover up his sin (see II Sam. 11). For at least a year, David continued to deceive everyone. However, he could not hide his sin from God. His deception only led to greater suffering.

After describing David's terrible sin, the Bible simply states, "But the thing that David had done displeased the Lord" (v. 27). However, this is not the end of the story. The Lord sent Nathan the prophet to David. Imagine for a moment that you are Nathan. You must go to your king and confront him with his terrible sins of adultery and murder, both of which have been complicated by deception. You know that David has a quick temper. You think to yourself, *What if the king becomes angry with me? He can have me banished or even killed.* Nathan faced a dilemma. Even though David was a sinner, he was also the sovereign. He had complete control and could do whatever he wished with Nathan, just as he had done with Bathsheba and Uriah. If you had been Nathan, what would you have done?

It's interesting to see how Nathan handled this situation. He knew that, in spite of David's sins, the king still had a childlike spirit. So the prophet

treated David like a disobedient and stubborn child,
appealing to his childlike spirit through the use of a
story. Nathan first drew a picture for David, then
turned that picture into a mirror so David could see
himself, and then made the mirror a window
through which David could see the Lord and seek
forgiveness. Let's consider this threefold approach
used by Nathan and see how it applies to our lives
today.

The Picture

In dealing with sin in our lives and in the lives of
others, it is vital that we first bring the sin out into
the open, for the Bible tells us, "He that covereth his
sins shall not prosper: but whoso confesseth and
forsaketh them shall have mercy" (Prov. 28:13).
David had been covering his sin, and so Nathan first
showed David a picture designed to touch his emotions and to remind him of his unconfessed sin.
"And the Lord sent Nathan unto David. And he
came unto him, and said unto him, There were two
men in one city; the one rich, and the other poor.
The rich man had exceeding many flocks and
herds: but the poor man had nothing, save one little
ewe lamb, which he had bought and nourished up:
and it grew up together with him, and with his
children; it did eat of his own meat, and drank of his
own cup, and lay in his bosom, and was unto him as
a daughter. And there came a traveller unto the rich
man, and he spared to take of his own flock and of
his own herd, to dress for the wayfaring man that
was come unto him; but took the poor man's lamb,

and dressed it for the man that was come to him. And David's anger was greatly kindled against the man; and he said to Nathan, As the Lord liveth, the man that hath done this thing shall surely die: and he shall restore the lamb fourfold, because he did this thing, and because he had no pity" (II Sam. 12:1-6).

Nathan's story deeply touched David's emotions, not only because it painted a picture of extreme cruelty and greed but also because it brought to light his own guilt. This story revealed three important truths about David. First, it revealed *how David sinned.*

Although David didn't see the connection at first between Nathan's story and his own sin, the meaning of the story is clear. David was the rich man, and Uriah was the poor man. The much-loved ewe lamb represented Bathsheba. The traveler in the story stood for temptation. Temptation came to David's house like a traveler. Instead of turning this guest away, he chose to invite temptation in and entertain it. David had made his first mistake when he left the battlefield and returned to Jerusalem alone. One night he took a walk along the roof of the palace. Looking down, he saw his neighbor's wife bathing. At that moment temptation came knocking at the door. Rather than turning it away, David chose to entertain his lust. Before long this guest became a friend, and David gave in to the temptation to send for this woman and lie with her (see 11:1-4). From then on, this friend was no longer a traveler but a permanent guest and master. One sin led to another, and soon David was being controlled by this temptation.

Like David, we are constantly faced with temptations that come to our door. If we open the door of our imagination and our heart to this traveler, he will come in as a guest. Soon we will start to entertain the possibility of disobeying God. Before long this guest becomes our friend, and we become comfortable with sin. Once this happens, our friend called sin will become our master.

In addition, this story is a picture that tells us *why David sinned.* He sinned because he had forgotten the goodness of God. The Lord had been good to David. In I Samuel 12, Nathan reminded David of everything the Lord had done for him. God had saved David from Saul's treachery. He had made David king and had given him all the house of Israel and Judah. And if all this had not been enough, the Lord would have given him much more (see vv. 7,8). David was a rich man with many wives and possessions. He should have said, "I have plenty. I don't need to rob someone else." But, instead, David robbed Uriah of his wife's loyalty and purity, and then he even robbed Uriah of his life.

Because David forgot the goodness of God, he also forgot about his sin, for it is the goodness of God that leads us to repentance (see Rom. 2:4). After the Prodigal Son had squandered his inheritance and was living in poverty, he remembered the goodness of his father and it softened his hard heart. He said, "How many hired servants of my father's have bread enough and to spare, and I perish with hunger!" (Luke 15:17). This son repented of his sin and went home, where he was forgiven and restored.

When David saw Uriah's wife, he should have said, "Yes, this woman is very beautiful and desirable, but I won't allow myself to desire her. I have a loyal family and a good home. I have so many wonderful blessings. I don't need anything else. God has given me all that I need." Dwelling on the goodness of God and the blessings He has given you is one of the best ways to fight temptation. When the Devil baits his hook, saying, "Don't you know that the Lord is holding out on you? If God really loved you, He would give you what I'm offering you," you need to stop and realize how good God has been to you. The writer James was referring to this principle when he wrote: "Every man is tempted, when he is drawn away of his own lust, and enticed. Then when lust hath conceived, it bringeth forth sin: and sin, when it is finished, bringeth forth death. Do not err, my beloved brethren. Every good gift and every perfect gift is from above, and cometh down from the Father of lights" (James 1:14-17). Remembering the goodness of God will keep you from rushing into sin.

From this picture we discover not only how David sinned (he entertained temptation) and why he sinned (he forgot the goodness of God and therefore despised God's Word) but also *what the sin did to him.* David's sin blinded him to himself. We find his reaction to Nathan's story in II Samuel 12:5: "And David's anger was greatly kindled against the man." From this passage I get the impression that the king thought Nathan was bringing him an actual civil suit that had to be settled. David didn't see himself in this story; he saw someone else. Whenever we're hiding sin in our lives, it always blinds us to ourselves.

Because this is true, Christ's warning about judging others is even more important. He told us, "Judge not, that ye be not judged. For with what judgment ye judge, ye shall be judged: and with what measure ye mete, it shall be measured to you again" (Matt. 7:1,2). This is exactly what happened to David. David passed judgment on the man in Nathan's story, saying, "As the Lord liveth, the man that hath done this thing shall surely die: and he shall restore the lamb fourfold, because he did this thing, and because he had no pity" (II Sam. 12:5,6). In his judgment, David was meting out the punishment for stealing that had been instituted in the Law: "If a man shall steal an ox, or a sheep, and kill it, or sell it; he shall restore five oxen for an ox, and four sheep for a sheep" (Ex. 22:1).

However, in doing so, David sealed his own judgment. Even though he deserved to die for the adultery and murder he had committed, God spared David's life. However, he was ultimately required to restore fourfold. But how could he do this? How could he give Bathsheba's husband back to her? How could he give Bathsheba's purity back to her? While he couldn't restore what had been lost, David was required to repay fourfold with the lives of his children. First, the baby that had been conceived in adultery to David and Bathsheba died (see II Sam. 12:15-19). Then Amnon violated his sister Tamar and was subsequently murdered by his brother Absalom for his crime (see 13:1-32). Later, when Absalom tried to usurp the throne of his father, he was killed by David's captain, Joab (see 18:9-15). Then still another son, Adonijah, tried to take the throne from the chosen successor, Solomon, and was executed (see I Kings 2:13-25). Because of his sin and self-proclaimed judgment, David saw his sins repeated in his own sons. What a price to pay!

The Mirror

As David listened to Nathan's story, he saw a picture of someone else's sin. But then Nathan turned the story around so that it became a mirror that reflected David's own sins. Once the king had passed judgment on the man, Nathan told him, "Thou art the man" (II Sam. 12:7). What courage it took for the prophet to say this! Anyone who has tried to point out a person's sin to him knows how Nathan felt. Confronting fellow believers is one of the hardest tasks of the Christian life. But it is a necessary task. Because we frequently have difficulty recognizing problems in our own lives, we should welcome loving criticism from others. However, all too often we respond with anger and bitterness toward the person who is trying to help us.

While David sinned grievously in his adulterous relationship with Bathsheba, we do credit him with taking an honest look at himself in the mirror that

Nathan gave him and with truly repenting of his sin. As David looked into this mirror, what did he see? First, he saw *a man who had experienced God's goodness.* In pointing out David's sin to him, the prophet first reminded him of everything the Lord had done for him: "Thus saith the Lord God of Israel, I anointed thee king over Israel, and I delivered thee out of the hand of Saul; and I gave thee thy master's house, and thy master's wives into thy bosom, and gave thee the house of Israel and of Judah; and if that had been too little, I would moreover have given unto thee such and such things" (vv. 7,8). As David looked at himself, he realized how ungrateful he had been for the tremendous blessings he had received from God.

The mirror also revealed to David *a man who had despised God's Word.* Even though David had been able to hide his sin from those around him, he could not hide it from God. Nathan reminded him vividly of his long-hidden sin, asking him, "Wherefore hast thou despised the commandment of the Lord, to do evil in his sight? thou hast killed Uriah the Hittite with the sword, and hast taken his wife to be thy wife, and hast slain him with the sword of the children of Ammon" (v. 9). David knew God's commandments forbidding murder and adultery, yet he chose to reject His Word. And the Lord made it clear that despising His Word is the same as despising Him. The Lord told David, "Now therefore the sword shall never depart from thine house; because thou hast despised me" (v. 10).

Not only did David see a man who had despised

God's Word, but he also saw *a man who had disgraced God's name*. The prophet told David, "Howbeit, because by this deed thou hast given great occasion to the enemies of the Lord to blaspheme" (v. 14). The Lord's name was dragged down in disrepute because of what David had done. Israel's unbelieving neighbors saw how Israel's king behaved and assumed that God was no different from their own gods. Because David had disgraced God's name, he would spend the rest of his life living in shame as well. The Lord told David that while he had taken Uriah's wife in secret, his neighbors would commit adultery with David's wives in public. While David had used devious methods to have Uriah killed, all Israel would see his sons murdered (see vv. 10-13).

David discovered how painful a close examination of himself in the mirror of God's Word can be. But when he was forced to look closely at himself in the mirror, he saw what kind of a person he really was. He saw a man who had experienced God's goodness and yet was ungrateful. He saw a man who had despised God's Word and was unyielding. And he saw a man who had disgraced God's name and had hurt God's people. But without this examination, David never would have reached the place of repentance and forgiveness.

Like David, we need to take a good look at ourselves in the mirror of God's Word. All too often we just stop to glance at ourselves, merely hearing the Word but not applying it to our lives. Soon we begin to overlook our faults and sins and to develop a self-righteous attitude. We must not only read the Word but also apply it daily to our lives in order to discover the sins that would hinder our relationship with the Lord and disgrace His name (see James 1:22-25). How long has it been since you looked at yourself closely in this mirror?

The Window

When we examine ourselves closely in the mirror of God's Word, earnestly looking for any sin in our lives, then this mirror becomes a window through which we can see God and go to Him for forgiveness and healing. As David came face to face with his sin, he humbly and sorrowfully confessed, "I have sinned against the Lord" (II Sam. 12:13). Nathan's response indicates that David's remorse over his sin and his subsequent confession were genuine. Nathan told David that he had been forgiven by God: "The Lord also hath put away thy sin; thou shalt not die" (v. 13).

We see here a tremendous example of God's grace. Adultery and murder were capital crimes according to the Law. Justice demanded that David be executed. However, because David expressed true repentance for his sins, he was pardoned by God. However, David also experienced God's government. Even though God had forgiven his sin and took away the penalty of it, David still had to suffer the consequences of pardoned sin. He spent the rest of his life reaping what he had sown. He saw his sons and his neighbors violate his wives and daughters. He saw his sons rebel against him and

53

try to take the kingdom away from him. And he experienced the grief of having four sons die because of his sin.

Have you ever noticed how all the good things in life are paid for in advance? For example, if you want to enjoy good music, you spend time and money learning how to play an instrument. Learning a trade also requires time and discipline. The same is true in learning how to live for God. However, we pay for the sin in our lives on the installment plan—even sins that God has forgiven. While our sin may seem harmless at the time, we always pay for it later. Galatians 6:7,8 tells us, "Be not deceived; God is not mocked: for whatsoever a man soweth, that shall he also reap. For he that soweth to his flesh shall of the flesh reap corruption; but he that soweth to the Spirit shall of the Spirit reap life everlasting."

When David looked at the picture that Nathan painted for him, his anger erupted at the sin of another person. But then that picture turned into a mirror, and David realized that he was looking at his own sin. Instead of becoming angry at Nathan or blaming others for his sin, David faced himself and his sin squarely and confessed it to God. As he did, this mirror became a window through which he saw the grace of God being extended to him. He heard the most welcome words ever uttered: "The Lord also hath put away thy sin; thou shalt not die" (II Sam. 12:13). One translation renders this passage: "The Lord has laid thy sin on another." What a beautiful picture of what God has done for us through Jesus Christ! He has laid on Him the iniquity of us all (Isa. 53:6).

Is our anger at others a "cover up" for our own sins?

"He that covereth his sins shall not prosper: but whoso confesseth and forsaketh them shall have mercy" (Prov. 28:13).

Chapter 5

Elisha: Angry at Missed Opportunities

What is your church's greatest treasure? Financial resources? Large facilities? While these are both good, unless God's people have true faith and vision, they will miss many opportunities for greater service and growth.

The Prophet Elisha became angry at the king of Israel because he limited himself and, as a result, also limited what God would do for him and for the nation. In II Kings 13 we read: "Now Elisha was fallen sick of his sickness whereof he died. And Joash the king of Israel came down unto him, and wept over his face, and said, O my father, my father, the chariot of Israel, and the horsemen thereof. And Elisha said unto him, Take bow and arrows. And he took unto him bow and arrows. And he said to the king of Israel, Put thine hand upon the bow. And he put his hand upon it: and Elisha put his hands upon the king's hands. And he said, Open the window eastward. And he opened it. Then Elisha said, Shoot. And he shot. And he said, The arrow of the Lord's deliverance, and the arrow of deliverance from Syria: for thou shalt smite the Syrians in Aphek, till thou have consumed them.

"And he said, Take the arrows. And he took them. And he said unto the king of Israel, Smite upon the ground. And he smote thrice, and stayed [stopped]. And the man of God was wroth [angry] with him, and said, Thou shouldest have smitten five or six times; then hadst thou smitten Syria till thou hadst consumed it: whereas now thou shalt smite Syria but thrice" (vv. 14-19).

For years, Hazael, the king of Syria, had been attacking the nations of Israel and Judah. When Hazael had taken Gath and was on his way to Jerusalem, the king of Judah had stripped the temple of the gold and dedicated objects and had sent them, along with his own treasures, to Hazael as a peace offering (see 12:17,18). Because the Lord was angry at the nation of Israel for their many sins, they were being oppressed even more by Hazael and his son Ben-hadad (see 13:3). Thus, when Joash, the king of Israel, heard that God's prophet, Elisha, was dying, he became worried. He went to Elisha, hoping to receive some blessing before the prophet died. And Elisha did indeed give Joash and his army God's blessing and promise of victory over Syria.

However, in doing so, Elisha also tested the faith of Joash and found him lacking. King Joash was a man who limited himself. Because he did not have the vision to ask great things of God, he did not receive all the blessings that God wanted to give him. In examining the life of King Joash, we discover that he had four limitations. Many people today place similar limitations on themselves and on God. We need to be aware of these limitations so that we can avoid making the same mistakes in our lives and our churches that Joash made.

Limited Appreciation for God's Servant

Joash missed opportunities for even greater blessing by God because he had a limited appreciation for God's servant. He did not recognize what kind of a man Elisha really was. Elisha was a man who exhibited great boldness and bravery. He had also been given special blessings and power from the Lord. He had been called by Elijah the prophet to be his successor. When Elijah was taken into heaven by a whirlwind, Elisha had the privilege of witnessing it, indicating that he would receive a double portion of Elijah's spirit (see II Kings 2:1-13).

God worked mightily through Elisha and gave him a long, fruitful ministry. Elisha ministered during the reigns of five different kings in the Northern Kingdom. The Bible records 20 different miracles performed by Elisha, including one that took place after his death and burial (see 13:20,21). For example, Elisha displayed power over nature. God enabled him to part the Jordan River (2:14) and to purify water that was polluted (vv. 19-22). He multiplied the widow's oil so she could pay her bills and keep her children from being sold into slavery (4:1-7). Elisha also possessed power over disease and death. He healed Naaman of his leprosy (5:1-14) and even raised a young boy from the dead (4:18-37). In addition, Elisha made a number of prophecies, including Israel's defeat of the Moabites (3:10-27). Indeed, Elisha was a man who was powerfully used by God. He was a great man of prayer. We would think that the various kings of Israel and Judah would have continually sought Elisha's wisdom and fellowship. It seems only natural that they would have appreciated him and depended upon him.

However, this was not the case. The kings did not appear to consult Elisha except when they were in a seemingly impossible situation (see 3:4-14). They did not desire to know the word of the Lord and often persecuted Elisha and the other prophets when God sent them with a message. But when Elisha was about to die, it is interesting to see who soon shows up to see him—Joash (also known as Jehoash), the king of Israel. Joash weeps by the bed of Elisha, saying, "O my father, my father, the chariot of Israel, and the horsemen thereof" (13:14).

Joash didn't recognize Elisha's role as the spiritual father of Israel until the prophet was about to die. Elisha had been caring for the people, feeding them generously from the Word of God and warning them about sin. He was doing everything a father does. He nourished, protected and taught the Children of Israel. Yet, it appears that the king hadn't followed Elisha's leadership or appreciated his ministry until it was too late.

Isn't this what so often happens in our lives? We take our parents, grandparents and other relatives and friends for granted. Then they are stricken with a terminal illness or are in a terrible accident. Sud-

59

denly, they become very important to us, and we give them special attention and treatment. Why don't we treat people every day as though this were the last day we might see them?

King Joash not only had ignored the spiritual leadership of Elisha, but he had not recognized before what a key role Elisha played in Israel's military victories. Joash finally realized that, without Elisha's intervention before God in their behalf, the nation would have perished long ago. The Lord, through Elisha, had brought deliverance to the people on more than one occasion. The king told the prophet that he was more important to the nation than all the chariots and horsemen of Israel.

What is a church's greatest asset? It is not its building nor its buses nor its budgets but rather its godly people—people who walk with the Lord, who know the truth of God, who know how to pray. As Christians, we should desire to live in such a way that our contributions to our nation, our church and our family will be missed after we are gone.

This final incident in the life of Elisha also shows us that our work for the Lord is never finished until the moment we take our final breath on earth. Even on his deathbed, the elderly prophet was still displaying the power of God. He prophesied Israel's defeat of Syria, telling the king to take the bow and arrows and to shoot an arrow out the window to the east. In the Old Testament era, when you wanted to declare war on another nation, it was a common practice to shoot an arrow into the enemy's territory. Since Syria was located east of Israel, Elisha was demonstrating to Joash that the Lord would give them victory in their war with the Syrians. Not only did Elisha prophesy, but he laid his dying hands on the king's hands, giving Joash the power and blessing of the Lord that would enable him to accomplish this victory.

We can learn another important lesson from Elisha. Even though he was dying, he was still thinking about others. He could have easily felt sorry for himself, thinking, *Why didn't God take me home the way he took Elijah? Why do I have to endure this pain and suffering? Why do I have to die when Elijah didn't?* But Elisha understood that God has different plans for different people. So instead of questioning God or wallowing in self-pity and depression, Elisha spent his last days on earth thinking about others and serving the Lord. The prophet showed a genuine concern for the king and for his nation. He was grieved over the situation with the Syrians and wanted to do what he could to help. So once again, he allowed himself to be the instrument God used to proclaim His message of deliverance.

Elisha had been faithfully serving the Lord and the nation of Israel for about 60 years, yet Joash didn't recognize and appreciate this servant of God until it was too late. What about you? Have you told your pastor lately that you appreciate his ministry and that you pray for him daily? Have you told your aged relative that you love him and thank God for him? Let's show appreciation to the people of God and thank the Lord for them while we still can.

Limited Understanding of God's Will

Not only did King Joash not appreciate the ministry of Elisha until it was too late, but he also had a limited understanding of God's will. Elisha's instructions and prophecy were clear. He told Joash to shoot an arrow out the window, signifying Israel's challenge to battle. Then the prophet instructed him, "Take the arrows. . . . Smite upon the ground" (II Kings 13:18). Some translations render this passage, "Shoot into the ground." Joash obeyed, but he only did it three times, revealing that he did not really grasp God's plan. The arrows represented the victory that God was going to give the king. The number of times Joash struck the ground—or shot the arrows into the ground—would determine how many victories he would receive.

The meaning of Elisha's prophecy should have been clear to Joash. But the king had no spiritual discernment. He had a limited understanding of the will of God because he probably had a limited understanding of God Himself.

It's a tragedy when Christians cannot see what God is doing in their lives. It's especially tragic when we face a crisis with no understanding of what God wants to accomplish. Moses is an illustration to us of a man who knew what God was doing because God clearly revealed it to him. Psalm 103:7 tells us, "He made known his ways unto Moses, his acts unto the children of Israel." Because Moses had a close relationship with the Lord, he not only saw *what* the Lord was doing but he also knew *why* He

62

was doing it. He understood God's will because he was directly involved in carrying it out. The Children of Israel, on the other hand, were merely spectators. They saw the acts but did not really understand the reasons behind them. In this way, they were like Joash.

Unfortunately, too many believers today are armchair Christians. They sit back and watch God work in their lives and in the lives of others without being able to understand His purposes. Why? Because they haven't learned enough about the Lord and His Word to understand His principles. They have failed to develop an intimate relationship with Him that would lead to understanding His will and His ways of working. Therefore, they fall apart when a crisis comes and begin to accuse God of not caring about them.

How sad it is when we have a limited understanding of God's will. We need to constantly pray, "Teach me Thy will, Lord." We must read and meditate on the Word of God in order to discover the mind of God. The Apostle Paul knew the importance of knowing God's will. Therefore, he prayed for the Ephesians: "That the God of our Lord Jesus Christ, the Father of glory, may give unto you the spirit of wisdom and revelation in the knowledge of him: the eyes of your understanding being enlightened; that ye may know what is the hope of his calling, and what the riches of the glory of his inheritance in the saints, and what is the exceeding greatness of his power to us-ward who believe" (Eph. 1:17-19). In other words, Paul was saying, "Oh,

God, open the eyes of their hearts that they might see what You have done, what You are doing and what You will continue to do for those who trust You."

Limited Faith in God's Power

King Joash had a limited appreciation of God's servant, Elisha. He also had a limited understanding of God's will. Joash went through the motions, but he did not really know why he was doing it. Joash had still a third limitation that prevented him from using the opportunities presented to him. He had a limited faith in God's power.

Elisha had good reason to become angry at Joash. He had bluntly told the king exactly what was going to happen. "The arrow of the Lord's deliverance, and the arrow of deliverance from Syria: for thou shalt smite the Syrians in Aphek, till thou have consumed them" (II Kings 13:17). Joash had God's promise of victory. However, he did not claim the Lord's promise by faith. He underestimated the power of God. Elisha told Joash that if he had really believed God, he would have beaten the ground five or six times rather than merely three. Therefore, Joash's victory was limited by his faith.

No doubt Elisha died a disappointed man. He had spent his life ministering to the Children of Israel, trying to bring them back to God. When the king showed so little faith, Elisha probably wondered if the people had heard anything he had said. He may have questioned, "Is there any faith left in Israel?"

God responds to our faith. In healing two blind

64

men, Jesus told them, "According to your faith be it unto you" (Matt. 9:29). Faith either releases God's power or limits God's power. When we have true faith, nothing is impossible (see 17:20). However, the Lord limits His work when unbelief is present (see 13:58). He leaves the choice up to us. He will only empower us to the degree that we want to be empowered.

Limited Victory in God's Service

Because Joash had a limited understanding of God's will and a limited faith in His power, he experienced a limited victory in God's service. In II Kings 13:25 we are told, "And Jehoash [Joash] the son of Jehoahaz took again out of the hand of Ben-hadad the son of Hazael the cities, which he had taken out of the hand of Jehoahaz his father by war. Three times did Joash beat him, and recovered the cities of Israel." Why was Joash successful only three times? Because he had already decided the matter when he had struck the ground with the arrows three times. The Lord only gave him what he had asked for.

We find an important principle at work here. Public victories are based on private victories. Before David met Goliath on the battlefield and killed him in full view of both armies, he had already killed a lion and a bear while herding his sheep alone in the hills. Before Jesus suffered public humiliation and death on the cross, He had already surrendered His life privately in the Garden of Gethsemane. Our outward actions are merely a reflection

65

of our inward attitudes. If we are not walking with God privately, then our public service will be limited and ineffectual.

Even though we have God's promise of complete victory through Jesus Christ (see I Cor. 15:57), many Christians are experiencing only partial victories because their own spiritual lives are sadly lacking. They are not meeting God privately each day to commune with Him. They are not acting by faith on the promises found in God's Word. Yet, they blame the Lord for their failures when they are really at fault. Oh, the tragedy of lost opportunity!

Because King Joash failed privately, he limited himself publicly. He could have defeated the Syrians completely. However, he chose to limit God's power and ignore God's will. As a result, the whole nation of Israel suffered from Syrian oppression in the years to come.

Joash had four serious limitations in his life that caused him to miss the opportunities God wanted to give him for victory. He had a limited appreciation of God's servant, Elisha. He apparently had taken Elisha for granted until he thought the prophet was about to die. Only then did he realize how important Elisha was to the nation. Likewise, Joash had a limited understanding of God's will. Because the king's relationship with the Lord was not what it should have been, he didn't understand God's plan for defeating the Syrians. He merely went through the motions of obeying the Lord without knowing why he was doing it. This led to a limited faith in God's power. Joash underestimated what the Lord would do for him. Because he did not have the faith to claim God's promises, he experienced a limited victory in God's service. As a result, both he and the nation of Israel suffered.

The same is true in our lives and in our churches. When we place limitations on ourselves and on God, we are not the only ones who suffer. Churches grow weak when their members live on partial victories.

Elisha was justified in his anger over Joash's missed opportunities. We should be angry at ourselves and at others whenever we try to limit God. The Lord wants to give us great victories in His service, both for our blessing and for His glory. There is no limit to what we can do when we trust completely in our limitless God. He is "able to do exceeding abundantly above all that we can ask or think, according to the power that worketh in us" (Eph. 3:20). Nothing is impossible for God to do when we simply believe. Let's not limit Him by our ignorance and unbelief. Let's claim the promises of God and win His victories.

Chapter 6

Uzziah: Angry Because He Got Caught

Anger can be a wonderful tool in the hands of God, if the anger is holy and justified. However, selfish, sinful anger can be a terrible weapon in the hands of the Devil. Frequently selfish anger leads us to commit sins that hurt others. Cain's anger led to jealousy and eventually to murder. Likewise, four of David's sons died as a result of his anger, sin and punishment. However, even if our rage does not seriously harm others, sinful anger still hurts—and even destroys—us. In fact, the person who is angry is always hurt far more than those with whom he is angry.

We see this fact graphically illustrated in the life of King Uzziah. During the days of the Old Testament monarchy, the word of the king was law. The king held the power of life and death because he was God's deputy on earth. He was responsible for enforcing God's Law. Therefore, above all else, the people wanted to avoid making the king angry. They knew that the results could be deadly! In fact, God's Word repeatedly warned them against enraging the king. Proverbs 16:14 states, "The wrath of a king is as messengers of death: but a wise man will pacify it." Proverbs 20:2 adds, "The fear of a king is

68

as the roaring of a lion: whoso provoketh him to anger sinneth against his own soul." This placed a great responsibility not only on the people but also on the king. He had to make sure that his judgments were based solely on righteous anger toward a person's sin and not on his own selfish anger and pride.

In most cases, the king's anger—both righteous and sinful—had a direct effect on the people. However, in the case of King Uzziah, we find that his unholy anger only hurt himself. Second Chronicles 26 records this sad story of a good king gone bad—and its unhappy results: "And his name spread far abroad; for he was marvellously helped, till he was strong. But when he was strong, his heart was lifted up to his destruction: for he transgressed against the Lord his God, and went into the temple of the Lord to burn incense upon the altar of incense. And Azariah the priest went in after him, and with him fourscore priests of the Lord, that were valiant men: and they withstood Uzziah the king, and said unto him, It appertaineth not unto thee, Uzziah, to burn incense unto the Lord, but to the priests the sons of Aaron, that are consecrated to burn incense: go out of the sanctuary; for thou hast trespassed; neither shall it be for thine honour from the Lord God.

"Then Uzziah was wroth [angry], and had a censer in his hand to burn incense: and while he was wroth with the priests, the leprosy even rose up in his forehead before the priests in the house of the Lord, from beside the incense altar. And Azariah the chief priest, and all the priests, looked upon him, and, behold, he was leprous in his forehead, and

69

they thrust him out from thence; yea, himself hasted also to go out, because the Lord had smitten him. And Uzziah the king was a leper unto the day of his death, and dwelt in a several [separate] house, being a leper; for he was cut off from the house of the Lord: and Jotham his son was over the king's house, judging the people of the land" (vv. 15-21).

When you read the account of Uzziah's reign in II Kings 15:1-5 and II Chronicles 26, you discover that he was a highly successful and popular king who had faithfully followed the Lord for many years. Yet, here we find him blatantly sinning. He—of all people—should have known that only the priests could offer incense in the Holy Place. However, when the priests confronted him with his sin, King Uzziah did not repent but instead became angry at them. In fact, the Hebrew word for anger used in this passage literally means "to boil up, to storm." This word was often used in describing a raging sea. This was no mild anger; Uzziah was raging at the priests. He was having a temper tantrum in the house of God. What would cause this king, who had been so faithful, to become angry as he did? In looking closer at this incident, we find at the heart of his disobedience and anger a number of other sins—sins that every Christian can fall prey to unless he is very careful.

An Ungrateful Heart

Behind Uzziah's anger lay, first of all, the sin of an ungrateful heart. The Lord had blessed King Uzziah greatly, giving him a long and prosperous reign. And, apart from this particular sin, Uzziah has been remembered throughout history as a wise and faithful ruler. The Bible tells us, "He did that which was right in the sight of the Lord" (II Chron. 26:4).

God blessed Uzziah in a remarkable way because he truly sought the Lord's will for his life. "He sought God in the days of Zechariah, who had [gave] understanding in the visions of God" (v. 5). Zechariah (not to be confused with the one who wrote the Book of Zechariah) was one of the godly prophets of that time. Unlike many of the kings before him, Uzziah sought Zechariah's friendship and help in understanding the will of the Lord. Uzziah listened eagerly to the prophet's teachings from the Word of God and obeyed them to the best of his ability.

It also appears that Uzziah had a godly mother who may have instilled in him the faith to trust God. Her name, Jecoliah, means "Jehovah will enable." Since Uzziah was only 16 years old when he ascended to the throne of his father, Amaziah, his mother no doubt had a great influence on him and on his reign during the early years. Through the influence of his mother and his friend Zechariah, Uzziah sought to follow the Lord. As a result, "God made him to prosper" (v. 5).

One of the blessings Uzziah enjoyed was that of military strength and victory. In this passage we learn that King Uzziah had a vast army of 307,500 soldiers and 2600 officers at his command (see vv. 12,13). He also had an abundant supply of equipment—shields, spears, helmets, armor, bows

71

and slingshots (v. 14). In addition, his men had invented specialized equipment similar to catapults for guarding the walls and towers of the cities and for attacking others (v. 15). Not since the time of David had the nation of Judah had such a reputation for military strength. The Lord helped them defeat both the Philistines and the Arabians (see vv. 6,7). The Ammonites feared the Jewish army so much that they brought peace offerings to Uzziah. Their fame spread throughout the nations—even to Egypt itself (see v. 8).

King Uzziah also enjoyed success and prosperity at home. He initiated a number of building programs and dug many wells. He was also a successful husbandman who deeply loved the soil. He had huge herds of cattle and many farms and vineyards (see vv. 9,10). King Uzziah was not only a man who was greatly blessed by God, but he was also a man whose life seemed to be balanced. He was not only a man of battle but also a man of building. He was a man of peace as well as a man of war. He was a wise and just ruler whose name was honored by his friends and enemies alike. And Uzziah knew the source of his success—God alone. Yet, with each new victory, Uzziah became less grateful and more proud. He began to want something more.

Like Uzziah, the stronger and more powerful we become, the greater the temptation to become proud. We forget that our strength and prosperity has come from God. We begin to rely on our strength and to desire more and more. When we begin to become proud, we need to remember the

Lord's warning: "Pride goeth before destruction, and an haughty spirit before a fall" (Prov. 16:18).

An Unholy Ambition

One of the first symptoms of backsliding is that we lose our gratitude for God. We aren't grateful for what He is doing for us. And an ungrateful heart will lead to a second sin—an unholy ambition.

Ambition can be good if it is motivated by God's will, if it is obedient to God's Word, and if it leads to God's glory. The Christian should be ambitious to grow in the Lord and to seek additional opportunities for serving Him. Too many believers become comfortable and satisfied in their work for the Lord. They rest on their past accomplishments rather than continuing to do all they can for Him.

However, when our ambition is not motivated by God's will and by obedience to God's Word, then it is unholy and destructive. God had given Uzziah every blessing. He was a wealthy and powerful king. Yet, he was not satisfied with his position. He wanted to be a priest as well. He ignored God's laws concerning the priesthood and attempted to assert his authority.

The Bible is filled with examples of people who exercised unholy ambition. For instance, Nadab and Abihu, the sons of Aaron, wanted to have more authority in the tabernacle than they had been given. So they tried to offer incense on the altar using a strange fire. As a result, God sent fire from heaven to consume them (see Lev. 10:1,2).

In Numbers 16, we find another example. Dathan

and Abiram, the sons of Eliab, defied the authority of Moses. They said, "Who is Moses, that he should tell us what to do? He brought us out into this desert just to let us die!" (see v. 13). Once again, God's punishment of their unholy ambition was swift. The Lord caused the ground to open up and swallow these men and their followers (see vv. 31-33). Likewise, Miriam, the sister of Moses, complained because Moses had been made the highest leader of the Israelites. She felt she had as much authority as Moses had. She said, "Hath the Lord indeed spoken only by Moses? hath he not spoken also by us?" (12:2). As a result of her unholy desire for power, God struck Miriam with leprosy.

In the New Testament, the classic example of unholy ambition is a man named Diotrephes. In III John, we read: "I wrote unto the church: but Diotrephes, who loveth to have the preeminence among them, receiveth us not" (1:9). Because of his own desire for power and absolute authority in his church, Diotrephes rejected the Apostle John and anyone who associated with him, fearing that he would lose his position and influence in the church. Not only did Diotrephes refuse to receive John and the other leaders when they came to visit, but he disciplined any church member who welcomed these men. Diotrephes was practicing what he thought was separation; however, it was merely isolation. John condemned this kind of attitude: "Wherefore, if I come, I will remember his deeds which he doeth, prating against us with malicious words: and not content therewith, neither doth he himself receive the brethren, and forbiddeth them that would, and casteth them out of the church" (v. 10).

We must be careful not to have unholy ambition. This is what turned the angel Lucifer into Satan. He said to himself, "I will be like the most High" (Isa. 14:14). Whenever people begin looking for more authority, power, money and other things that are outside of the will of God, they will only find trouble for themselves and for others. We need to seek God's will for our lives and to make it our sole ambition to serve Him more. King Uzziah was blessed greatly by the Lord when he was serving Him alone. But then he began running ahead of God, wanting authority that he was not entitled to possess. As a result, Uzziah lost what authority and prestige he had.

An Unyielded Will

Because King Uzziah forgot the blessings he had received from God and was blinded by his unholy ambition for more power, he did not yield his will to the Lord. No doubt Uzziah was familiar with the laws concerning who could serve as a priest. God's Word had made it clear: "Therefore thou and thy sons with thee shall keep your priest's office for every thing of the altar, and within the vail; and ye shall serve: I have given your priest's office unto you as a service of gift: and the stranger that cometh nigh shall be put to death" (Num. 18:7). The Lord had given the priesthood to Aaron and his descendants. Only they could serve in the tabernacle and

75

temple. Yet, even though King Uzziah knew God's Law, he ignored God's will and did as he pleased. He had become so proud that he believed God would make an exception for him.

But we never find God making an exception to His commandments. Like Uzziah, King Saul thought he was above God's Law. He assumed the office of priest, offering a sacrifice for the people. The pronouncement of Saul's punishment was swift and final. His kingdom was taken away from him and from his descendants (see I Sam. 13:8-14).

In the Old Testament, we find only one example of a king who was also a priest—Melchizedek (see Gen. 14:18). His name means "king of righteousness." He was the king of Salem, which means "peace," and was described as "the priest of the most high God" (v. 18). Of course, Melchizedek ruled before God instituted the Levitical priesthood. He was not bound by the Law.

We find only two other descriptions of a king-priest in the Bible, and these are used in a spiritual sense. The first king-priest, of course, is Jesus Christ. He is described as a priest after the order of Melchizedek (see Heb. 6:20; chs. 7-10). He is also the King of kings (I Tim. 6:15). Jesus is the king of righteousness and of peace. Righteousness and peace have been joined together in the Lord Jesus Christ because of Calvary.

Because of what Christ has done for us, each believer is also a king and a priest. Revelation 1:5,6 tells us, "Unto him that loved us, and washed us from our sins in his own blood, and hath made us kings and priests unto God." Through Christ, we have been made a royal priesthood (see I Pet. 2:9).

King Uzziah wanted to start a royal priesthood, but this was not the will of God. Even when Uzziah was confronted with his sin, he still did not repent. Azariah and 80 other priests came to Uzziah in the temple and warned him not to sin by offering the incense. They begged him to leave quickly. But instead of repenting, the king became enraged at them (see II Chron. 26:19). Because Uzziah refused to yield his will to the Lord, he brought God's judgment upon himself.

An Unhappy Life

The life of King Uzziah is a perfect illustration of God's warning: "Let him that thinketh he standeth take heed lest he fall" (I Cor. 10:12). Here we find a man who had faithfully served God for most of his life. He had brought glory to the Lord and had been greatly blessed as a result. But then he allowed an ungrateful heart, an unholy ambition and an unyielded will to rob him of these blessings. His life from that time forward was filled with unhappiness and misery. Uzziah spent his declining years alone as a leper. I can think of no greater tragedy than when a believer who has served God for many years lives his final years in shame as a result of sin.

The results of Uzziah's sin were threefold. First, *he lost his health.* Because Uzziah refused to repent, he brought God's judgment on himself. He was immediately stricken with leprosy. According to the Law, anyone who interfered in the priest's ministry or even entered the areas of the temple reserved for the priests were to be put to death. However, the Lord, in His mercy, chose to spare Uzziah's life. He instead cut Uzziah off from the people and forced him to spend the rest of his life in isolation as a leper.

The second result was a natural outgrowth of the first. Because of his leprosy, *he lost his throne.* Technically, Uzziah was still the king. However, because lepers were not allowed to be near people, Uzziah had to turn control of his kingdom over to his son Jotham (see II Chron. 26:21).

Not only was Uzziah cut off from his people and his position, but also *he lost his privilege of going to the temple.* Uzziah had disobeyed the will of God by trying to penetrate into the very heart of the temple. As a result, he was cut off from every area of the house of the Lord (see v. 21).

King Uzziah had to learn the hard way what happens when we do not learn to control our anger. When confronted with the sin in his life, Uzziah displayed anger at the wrong people and for the wrong reasons. Instead of becoming angry at himself and at his sin, he lashed out at those who were trying to bring him back to the will of God. His pride and temper kept him from seeking God's forgiveness. If he had only repented, he could have avoided much unhappiness and heartache.

Uzziah had won many battles and conquered many cities, but his kingdom was worthless because he never learned to control the kingdom within. He did not understand the great truth of Proverbs

16:32: "He that is slow to anger is better than the mighty; and he that ruleth his spirit than he that taketh a city." Unless we can first learn to control our anger and other desires, we will never enjoy success in our Christian life. Proverbs 14:29 tells us, "He that is slow to wrath is of great understanding: but he that is hasty of spirit exalteth folly." How do we gain control of a short temper? By remembering and expressing gratitude for everything the Lord has given us, by directing our ambitions toward His purposes and by yielding our will to His will. Only then can we experience the inner strength and peace that will enable us to control the rage within us.

Chapter 7

Jonah: An Angry Preacher

Many people have the idea that anger is always a sign of strength. On the contrary, it can be an evidence of weakness and fear. In the Old Testament, we meet an angry preacher. According to the world's standards, this man had a successful ministry. However, in God's eyes, he was really a personal failure. That preacher, of course, was Jonah. He allowed his anger and animosity toward the Ninevites to destroy the joy and blessings of his ministry.

The story of Jonah is a familiar one. If the Book of Jonah had ended with chapter 3, verse 10, Jonah would have looked very successful. Even though he had rebelled against God's call in the beginning, he experienced a miraculous answer to prayer while inside the belly of a great fish. Not only was his life spared, but he saw a tremendous awakening take place in Nineveh as a result of his preaching. But even though it appeared that Jonah's attitude toward the Ninevites had changed, in his heart he still harbored anger and resentment toward them and toward the Lord.

It is possible to be in the place of God's choosing and still have a heart that is hard, angry and rebellious toward God. Even though Jonah knew how to pray and how to preach, and even though his theology was grounded solidly in God's Word, he still became angry when he did not get his own way with the Lord. "But it displeased Jonah exceedingly [that God had spared the city], and he was very angry. And he prayed unto the Lord and said, I pray thee, O Lord, was not this my saying, when I was yet in my country? Therefore I fled before unto Tarshish: for I knew that thou art a gracious God, and merciful, slow to anger, and of great kindness, and repentest thee of the evil" (Jon. 4:1,2).

Jonah had realized when God called him to go to Nineveh that the Lord would spare the people if they repented. He wanted the Ninevites to be destroyed, so he ran away from the Lord rather than preach to them. Finally, after Jonah learned that he couldn't hide from God, he reluctantly went to Nineveh. There Jonah's worst fears were realized as the people repented. Like a child who does not get what he wants, Jonah began to pout and to feel sorry for himself, saying, "Therefore now, O Lord, take, I beseech thee, my life from me; for it is better for me to die than to live" (v. 3). Notice how the Lord responded to Jonah's anger and self-pity: "Do you have good reason to be angry?" (v. 4, NASB). The Lord forced Jonah to focus on his reasons for being angry. If Jonah had been honest with himself, he would have seen that his anger was unjustified. He should have been happy for the Ninevites and excited that God allowed him to have a part in their repentance.

But the prophet was not ready to repent of his anger just yet. "So Jonah went out of the city, and sat on the east side of the city, and there made him a booth, and sat under it in the shadow, till he might see what would become of the city. And the Lord God prepared a gourd, and made it to come up over Jonah, that it might be a shadow over his head, to deliver him from his grief. So Jonah was exceeding glad of the gourd" (vv. 5,6). In the back of his mind, Jonah was probably still hoping that God would destroy the city. So, just in case, he left the city and built himself a shelter nearby so he could watch what happened. Despite Jonah's repeated disobedience and rebellion, we find the Lord still caring for his needs. He caused a large plant to grow immediately, providing shade for Jonah. Notice Jonah's reaction. Just a few short hours before, he had been *exceedingly displeased* (v. 1). Now he was *exceedingly glad* for the Lord's provision of this plant (v. 6). Jonah appears to have been controlled by his emotions.

The Lord also had another reason for providing this plant for Jonah. He used it to teach the prophet an important lesson about unjustified anger. "But God prepared a worm when the morning rose the next day, and it smote the gourd that it withered. And it came to pass, when the sun did arise, that God prepared a vehement east wind; and the sun beat upon the head of Jonah, that he fainted, and wished in himself to die, and said, It is better for me to die than to live" (vv. 7,8).

Jonah's reaction reveals to us an important truth

about anger. Anger, self-pity and depression usually go together. A person who is filled with anger (even if he expresses that anger) will often undergo periods of depression and self-pity. Frequently he does not even realize that anger is the cause of his depression.

While Jonah was sitting there feeling sorry for himself, the Lord spoke to him again, driving home the point of this object lesson. "And God said to Jonah, Doest thou well to be angry for the gourd? And he said, I do well to be angry, even unto death. Then said the Lord, Thou hast had pity on the gourd, for the which thou hast not laboured, neither madest it grow; which came up in a night, and perished in a night: and should not I spare Nineveh, that great city, wherein are more than sixscore thousand persons that cannot discern between their right hand and their left hand; and also much cattle?" (vv. 9-11). The Lord told Jonah, "If you can have compassion for a plant that you didn't even grow or tend, why can't I forgive the people of Nineveh, whom I created?"

Unfortunately, the story ends here. We don't know how Jonah responded to the Lord. We must draw our own conclusions. We can only hope that if there were a verse 12, it would read: "And Jonah repented and said, O Lord, forgive me for my anger. I will now go back into the city and finish my job."

Reading the Book of Jonah is similar to undergoing a psychiatric examination. What is your response to the experience of Jonah? Do you symphathize with his dilemma, saying, "I agree with you, Jonah. Those Ninevites were wicked people, and they deserved to die. Like you, I'm angry too. I'm angry that God is allowing wicked people to continue doing whatever they want in the world today"? Even though most of us would not want to be like Jonah, often we respond to the unsaved in much the same way as he did. Like Jonah, we can be overjoyed at some small, insignificant honor or material possession we receive, yet we cannot feel happy when our enemy is converted or feel sad at the sin in our life. Anger shifts the focus of our priorities from God to ourselves.

This is why it is so dangerous for the Christian to allow selfish anger to control his life. When we are angry, it is difficult for us to discern what kind of anger we are experiencing. We tend to convince ourselves that we are feeling righteous indignation when, in reality, we are merely expressing a godless, selfish, worldly kind of anger. When we give in to this kind of anger, the Lord cannot bless us.

The Reason for His Anger

Why did Jonah become angry at God for sparing the Ninevites? What were the results of his anger? Considering these and other aspects of Jonah's anger can help us learn how to deal with the anger in our lives.

What was Jonah's reason for becoming angry? Actually, the answer is very simple—incomplete surrender to God. In order to use us, the Lord must have control of every aspect of our being—our body, mind, will and heart. We must yield ourselves completely to Him. We can hold nothing back.

Throughout the Book of Jonah, we find the prophet holding out on God. But gradually the Lord gained control of the various aspects of Jonah's life. In chapter 1, God penetrated Jonah's mind, telling him, "Arise, go to Nineveh, that great city, and cry against it" (v. 2). But, at this point, the Lord did not have control of the rest of Jonah. Jonah's will refused to go to Nineveh. His heart agreed totally with this rebellion, and the two caused his body to run away from God. But try as he might, Jonah could not rid his mind of God's words to him.

In chapter 2, we find God using circumstances to bring Jonah to the place where he would surrender his will to Him. As Jonah lay in the belly of a great fish, he cried out to God: "I will sacrifice unto thee with the voice of thanksgiving; I will pay [what] I have vowed" (v. 9). Once the Lord had Jonah's will, his body soon followed. In chapter 3, we find Jonah's mind and will directing his body to go to Nineveh.

Yet even though Jonah obeyed the Lord and preached in Nineveh, he was still not totally controlled by God, for his heart was not in it. It seems incredible that Jonah could preach one of the greatest revival sermons in Old Testament history, yet hate the people to whom he was preaching. What a tragic illustration of the truth stated in I Corinthians 13:1: "Though I speak with the tongues of men and of angels, and have not charity [love], I am become as sounding brass, or a tinkling cymbal." We can be the greatest evangelist who ever lived, but if we do not have a heartfelt love for the people with whom we are sharing, our words will be empty and meaningless.

However, the results of Jonah's preaching teaches us another important lesson about our service: God will use His Word even if His servant is not all that he should be. Even though Jonah's heart was not in his ministry, the Lord blessed His Word anyway, and the people repented despite Jonah's efforts to hinder them. It is possible for the Lord to bless a ministry without blessing its minister. When our heart is not right with God, we will miss the many wonderful benefits that can come from our service. However, God can and does accomplish His work.

Without love, any sacrifice we make or service we perform is worthless: "And though I have the gift of prophecy, and understand all mysteries, and all knowledge; and though I have all faith, so that I could remove mountains, and have not [love], I am nothing. And though I bestow all my goods to feed the poor, and though I give my body to be burned, and have not [love], it profiteth me nothing" (vv. 2,3). Why is our ministry worthless without love? Because it cannot bless the person who's doing the ministering.

Even though Jonah had not given his heart to God and to the people, the Lord still chose to use Jonah's ministry to lead the people to repentance. He did so because of His great love for the people and His compassion for the innocent children of Nineveh. The Lord's final words to Jonah are interesting. He told Jonah, "And should not I spare Nineveh, that great city, wherein are more than sixscore thousand persons that cannot discern between their right hand and their left hand; and also much cattle?" (Jon. 4:11). It seems likely that the 120,000 persons that God was referring to here were young children who had not yet reached the age of accountability. They were not old enough to discern right from wrong.

If this interpretation is correct, then we can see how large the city of Nineveh actually was. It was described as a "great city" (v. 11). When you add the parents to this number, as well as older children and adults without children, the population of this city could have been close to a million. Many commentators estimate that the population of Nineveh was at least 600,000—a city about the size of San Francisco. In this passage, the Lord was trying to make Jonah see how many innocent and righteous people would have been killed if He had destroyed the entire city because of the wickedness of a few.

To show Jonah the depth of His compassion, the Lord even expressed His concern for the animals. He told Jonah, in effect, "If all these people die in judgment, who will take care of the animals?" Jonah did not have this kind of pity.

Jonah was unwilling to surrender himself completely to God because his views of his relationship with the Lord were erroneous. First, Jonah had a *wrong attitude toward God's will.* He thought that God's will was something you could take or leave—

not something to be obeyed without question. Thus, when the Lord called Jonah to go to Nineveh, the prophet made up his mind to ignore God's will and to do as he pleased. Jonah also had a *wrong attitude toward prayer.* He believed in praying only when he was in trouble and needed the Lord's help. To Jonah, prayer was simply a magic charm to get what he wanted. Likewise, Jonah had the *wrong attitude toward obedience.* He obeyed the Lord because he had to, not because he wanted to. His service was motivated by a sense of duty and of fear rather than from a genuine love for the Lord and for His people. Finally, Jonah had a *wrong attitude toward lost souls.* He did not love unbelievers. His lack of love revealed itself in his anger and hatred toward the Ninevites and in his anger toward God for not destroying them.

The Results of His Anger

No matter what reasons you may have for becoming angry—whether holy or unholy—you will always reap the consequences of your anger. If your anger is righteous and just, then the results will be constructive. However, if your anger is rooted in selfishness and an incomplete surrender to God—as Jonah's anger was—then it will only serve to tear down your Christian life. You always lose when you harbor anger against God and against His people.

Even if you are justified in your anger against a brother, harboring anger or seeking revenge against the person is not only wrong but also it often hurts you far more than it hurts him. We need to leave

88

judgment and punishment to God: "Dearly beloved, avenge not yourselves, but rather give place unto wrath: for it is written, Vengeance is mine; I will repay, saith the Lord" (Rom. 12:19).

When you look at the life of Jonah, you discover only one person who really suffered from his anger—Jonah himself. While his fellow passengers on the ship suffered temporary peril because of his disobedience (see Jon. 1:4-15) and while Jonah's anger may have hurt some in Nineveh, in the end only Jonah suffered real loss.

What were the results of Jonah's anger? First, *he lost his testimony.* When Jonah saw that the people had repented, he left the city. God had opened the door for ministry in Nineveh. Jonah should have been seizing the opportunity to pray with the people and to teach them about the true God. But, instead, we find Jonah leaving his place of ministry and sitting outside the city, thinking only of himself. Even if Jonah did repent after his encounter with God and go back into the city, no doubt he found it nearly impossible to teach effectively. The people would've found it hard to trust him after what they had seen.

Not only did Jonah lose his testimony, but *he also lost his love.* Jonah allowed anger and hatred to destroy his love for God and for other people. His anger caused him to isolate himself from the love and fellowship he needed to build him up. As he sat there brooding over his anger, he became more and more despondent. Self-pity and a sense of hopelessness soon set in, and Jonah wanted to die. He cried out, "O Lord, take, I beseech thee, my life from me; for it is better for me to die than to live" (4:3). Nothing makes a person feel more hopeless and lonely than when he allows anger to replace love in his life. Anger tears you apart inside, while love builds you up.

In addition, *Jonah lost God's guidance.* The Lord had a special plan for Nineveh, and Jonah was the key to that plan. However, the prophet resisted God's guidance. He ran from God's will. So the Lord had to deal with His servant. Then Jonah wanted to die rather than to complete the Lord's ministry. He lost God's guidance because he was too wrapped up in himself. *He also lost God's Word.* Once Jonah left the city, we do not find God giving him any new revelation. When the Lord spoke, it was only to rebuke Jonah for his anger. Likewise, *Jonah lost God's power in prayer.* He was praying only for himself. He showed no concern for the needs of others.

Because Jonah was no longer being guided by God, *he lost his sense of values.* I've often seen this happen when a person begins to be controlled by anger. Anger produces incomplete obedience to God. This, in turn, causes our values to become distorted. Little things take on giant proportions, and what is really significant seems of small value. Because of his disobedience and anger, Jonah became self-centered. He only valued what could benefit him. Jonah rejoiced over the simple plant that God sent to shade him, yet he refused to celebrate with the people of Nineveh over the revival they had experienced. Likewise, when the gourd died, Jonah wept over it. But he felt no sorrow for the lost souls in Nineveh. Why? Because he had forgotten what it was like to be lost. He had forgotten how the Lord had saved him from the belly of the fish.

In the life of Jonah, we see the consequences of a broken relationship with the Lord. Without the Word of God and prayer to guide him, *Jonah lost his faith and joy.* He wanted the Lord to destroy the city. He didn't have the faith to understand why God would spare it. Jonah's service in Nineveh was not motivated by love and faith but by anger and fear. He was serving the Lord with madness—not gladness (see Ps. 100:2). Like Jonah, a number of pastors, Sunday school teachers and other Christian workers today are not serving God out of gladness and joy. They don't minister because they love lost souls. They simply want to "let them have it," condemning these people for their sins in order to make them feel guilty and miserable.

The Remedy for His Anger

Instead of rejoicing with the people of Nineveh about their revival, Jonah became angry. Why? Because he had not surrendered himself completely to God. He had the wrong attitude toward God's will and toward the people of Nineveh. As a result, Jonah lost his fellowship with the Lord. He no longer had God's Word and prayer to guide him. His faith, love and joy were gone. And his testimony

91

to the people was destroyed—all because of unjustified anger.

What's the remedy for this kind of anger? A good dose of *honesty* and *humility!* Jonah first needed to be honest with God and with himself. Throughout the Book of Jonah, we find the prophet arguing with God. When the Lord called Jonah and told him to go to Nineveh, Jonah turned and ran the other way. Everything in the Book of Jonah obeys God except Jonah—the wind, the worm, the gourd, the great fish, even the lost people in Nineveh! When God did not destroy Nineveh, Jonah retorted, "I knew this would happen! You know these people deserve to die. Why won't You destroy them?" (see Jon. 4:2). Isn't this always what happens when we allow anger to rule us? Instead of admitting that we were wrong, we become defensive and argumentative. Like Jonah, we justify our feelings of anger and self-pity, saying, "I have good reason to be angry" (v. 9, NASB). Thus, the first step to overcoming our anger is to admit to ourselves and to God that we are angry without just cause.

But honesty is just the first step toward healing. We must also have humility. Jonah should have fallen on his face before God and said, "O Lord, I've learned my lesson. I disobeyed you before—and after—I came to Nineveh. Forgive me. Remove this anger and hatred from my heart. Help me to do Your will." Forgiveness and healing cannot take place until we willingly surrender ourselves completely to God. If we try to rid ourselves of the anger and malice inside us, we will fail miserably. Only

92

God can remove the hatred that lurks deep within us and replace it with a spirit of love and forgiveness through His Spirit. "The love of God is shed abroad in our hearts by the Holy Ghost which is given unto us" (Rom. 5:5). This kind of love is stronger than anger. When we allow ourselves to be God's channel of love to others, then we experience His love in a greater way in our own lives. And when we are loving and being loved, there is no room for anger.

Thus, the remedy for anger is to become like the God whom we represent. Jonah knew what kind of God he served, but he was not willing to give the complete surrender and obedience that was required to become like Him: "For I knew that thou art a gracious God, and merciful, slow to anger, and of great kindness" (Jon. 4:2). The Holy Spirit can replace our anger with God's love, mercy, patience and kindness when we surrender our total being—body, mind, heart and will—to Him.

Chapter 8

An Angry Army

We have all had people become angry with us at one time or another, but imagine having 100,000 men angry at you at the same time. Imagine also that they are soldiers skilled in the use of weapons. You can see the dilemma you would be facing. What would you do?

One man in the Bible found himself in this exact situation—Amaziah, the king of Judah. We read in II Chronicles 25:5-10: "Moreover Amaziah gathered Judah together, and made them captains over thousands, and captains over hundreds, according to the houses of their fathers, throughout all Judah and Benjamin: and he numbered them from twenty years old and above, and found them three hundred thousand choice men, able to go forth to war, that could handle spear and shield. He hired also an hundred thousand mighty men of valour out of Israel for an hundred talents of silver.

"But there came a man of God to him, saying, O king, let not the army of Israel go with thee; for the Lord is not with Israel, to wit, with all the children of

Ephraim. But if thou wilt go, do it, be strong for the battle: God shall make thee fall before the enemy: for God hath power to help, and to cast down. And Amaziah said to the man of God, But what shall we do for the hundred talents which I have given to the army of Israel? And the man of God answered, The Lord is able to give thee much more than this. Then Amaziah separated them, to wit, the army that was come to him out of Ephraim, to go home again: wherefore their anger was greatly kindled against Judah, and they returned home in great anger."

King Amaziah made a grave mistake in hiring the Israelite soldiers. He did not seek God's will and, as a result, created problems for himself and for the nation. He angered an entire army and was forced to deal with the consequences of their anger. Like Amaziah, often we create problem situations for ourselves, and then we try to take the easy way out of them. But, as we will see, there are no shortcuts to dealing with anger and the difficulties it creates.

The Object of Their Anger

As we consider this angry army, three questions come to mind. The answers to these questions give us God's instructions for dealing with our anger and with those who are angry at us.

First, with whom was the army of Israel angry? They were angry at the nation of Judah in general and at Amaziah, the king of Judah, in particular. As you will recall, the Israelite nation split following the death of Solomon and the ascension of his son Rehoboam to the throne. The tribes of Benjamin and Judah formed the Southern Kingdom called Judah. They continued the house and lineage of David and, for the most part, remained faithful to God. The other ten tribes comprised the Northern Kingdom of Israel. Unlike Judah, the nation of Israel fell into idolatry almost as soon as they split. They formed their own religion. The intervening years before they were taken into captivity were marked by great wickedness and unfaithfulness. Because of Israel's wickedness and other factors, the two nations were at odds with each other much of the time.

Why would Amaziah appeal to his enemy for help in fighting his war, especially when he knew that God did not approve of them? We find help in answering this question from II Chronicles 25:2: "And he [Amaziah] did that which was right in the sight of the Lord, but not with a perfect heart." While Amaziah followed the Lord, he was serving Him halfheartedly. The king's obedience to God was not everything it should have been. His faith often wavered, and he frequently tried to do things on his own.

God wants total obedience from His children, for He knows that anything less will only cause us grief. James 1:8 tells us, "A double minded man is unstable in all his ways." The Bible warns us against being double-minded, double-hearted or double-willed. In Matthew 6:19-21, Jesus told us, "Lay not up for yourselves treasures upon earth, where moth and rust doth corrupt, and where thieves break through and steal: but lay up for yourselves treasures in heaven, where neither moth nor rust doth corrupt, and where thieves do not break through nor steal: for where your treasure is, there will your heart be also." The Lord knew that when our heart is divided between our devotion to Him and our love of worldly possessions, the world will always win out in the end. That is why it is important for us to commit everything we have to Him.

Likewise, the Lord does not want servants whose minds are divided. In Matthew 6:22,23, Jesus added, "The light of the body is the eye: if therefore thine eye be single, thy whole body shall be full of light. But if thine eye shall be evil, thy whole body shall be full of darkness. If therefore the light that is in thee be darkness, how great is that darkness!" In this passage, Jesus was telling us that we cannot look in two directions at the same time. If we are trying to keep our eyes on Him and on the world, we will develop double vision. And double vision produces spiritual blindness. People with divided minds become ineffective because it is impossible for them to give their complete attention to anything.

In this passage, the Lord Jesus also warned us against being double-willed: "No man can serve two masters: for either he will hate the one, and love the other; or else he will hold to the one, and despise the other. Ye cannot serve God and mammon" (v. 24). Many people today have divided loyalties. They are trying to serve the Lord and the world at the same time. But this never works. We must make a choice, for if we try to serve both, the world will always win out. Choosing to follow Christ involves a total

97

commitment—our whole heart, mind and will. We cannot be halfhearted in our Christian life and survive.

Amaziah's mind was divided. He was looking both to the Lord and to others for help. Likewise, instead of wholeheartedly trusting God for the victory, he put his faith in numerical strength and in money. Amaziah had 300,000 soldiers with which to fight the Edomites. With the Lord's help, he could have won with far fewer soldiers. But Amaziah put his faith in numbers instead of in God. So he hired another 100,000 mercenaries from the enemy, Israel, paying them a hundred talents of silver. He said to himself, *I have enough money to win this war.* Like so many people, Amaziah relied on human power and resources to solve his problems.

Notice Amaziah's response when the man of God told him that he must send the soldiers from Israel home because they did not have the Lord's blessing: "But what shall we do for the hundred talents which I have given to the army of Israel?" (II Chron. 25:9). The king was not asking himself, *Is this what God wants me to do?* but rather *Can I afford it?* The money was obviously more important to him than obedience.

When people start counting the cost of obedience, they are heading for trouble. Jesus made this fact perfectly clear: "It came to pass, that, as they went in the way, a certain man said unto him, Lord, I will follow thee whithersoever thou goest. And Jesus said unto him, Foxes have holes, and birds of the air have nests; but the Son of man hath not where to lay his head. And he said unto another, Follow me. But he said, Lord, suffer me first to go and bury my father. Jesus said unto him, Let the dead bury their dead: but go thou and preach the kingdom of God. And another also said, Lord, I will follow thee; but let me first go bid them farewell, which are at home at my house. And Jesus said unto him, No man, having put his hand to the plough, and looking back, is fit for the kingdom of God" (Luke 9:57-62). These men missed the blessing of following Jesus into His wonderful ministry because they were not willing to pay the price of obedience.

This incident in Amaziah's life also shows us the cost of disobedience. He knew that he should not have hired the soldiers from Israel, but he wanted victory more than obedience. As a result, he suffered tremendous financial loss, not to mention an even greater spiritual one. Scholars disagree on exactly how much a talent of silver was worth in that day, but many estimate that Amaziah's 100 talents of silver would have been worth more than $2 million. One study Bible lists the amount at $2,184,000. Amaziah could not retrieve that money since he had already paid the soldiers. By sending them home, he did not even receive the service return from his investment. You may be thinking to yourself, *How could someone be so foolish? Amaziah should have known that disobedience doesn't pay, that no amount of money can cover our sins!* Yet how much have we spent to cover our disobedience or to get our own way?

Amaziah made a mistake by hiring this army. And when he was confronted with his sin, he should have simply sent the army home and forgotten about the money. While he did reluctantly dismiss the soldiers, he still worried about his money instead of trusting God to supply his needs. The man of God told the king, "The Lord is able to give thee much more than this" (II Chron. 25:9).

Even though we must pay a price for our disobedience—suffering financial, physical, emotional or some other loss—we should not dwell on the mistakes of the past. Once we have confessed them, we need to forget about them and trust God to help us in the future. Obedience and disobedience both require an investment on our part. But the Lord's dividends for obedience far outweigh the temporary pleasures of disobedience.

The Reason for Their Anger

It seems strange that the Israelite soldiers became angry at Amaziah for sending them home. After all, they received their pay without having to earn it. We would think that they would have been glad to escape the rigors and dangers of battle. Why were they angry? I believe that a number of factors were involved.

The first reason for their anger was *pride.* They had been embarrassed publicly, and nobody likes to be embarrassed. When the king dismissed them, no doubt the rumors started to fly. The people may have been saying, "Why aren't they living up to their agreement? What kind of soldiers are they anyway?

I heard that the man of God told the king to send them home because the Lord was not with Israel. They would have only caused us trouble. After all, Israel is our enemy, you know. They would have probably turned traitor in the middle of the battle." When our pride is injured, our first response is to lash back in anger. We become defensive and vengeful. As we will see, this is exactly how these Israelite soldiers responded (see II Chron. 25:13).

A second reason for their anger was *selfishness*. These men were mercenaries. They were fighting simply for the money. They were not concerned at all about Judah or its cause. If the Edomites had offered them 200 talents of silver, they would have deserted Amaziah and his army in an instant and fought for the other side. Even though they had each received a large sum of money for those days, they wanted more. For a soldier, one of the benefits of war was being able to take the spoils after the battle. While he had to give the king a portion of whatever he took, he could still make quite a bit of money from plundering. Thus, these soldiers became angry because they were being denied the spoils of war. So they went out and plundered Judah instead (see v. 13).

It's amazing what people will do just to make money! Everywhere we look today, we find people whose only goal in life is to become as rich as they can. They will do whatever it takes to make a profit, reasoning that the end justifies the means. They will step on anyone they have to in order to reach the top. They have no standards or morals. But while they are making a **living**, they are not making a **life**. Often those who reach the top find nothing waiting there for them. This is why we see so many miserable, lonely and hopeless people in our world today. They have not yet learned that only Christ can give them true riches and satisfaction.

It is also likely that *nationalism* was involved in the anger of these soldiers. These soldiers were Israelites. Their country had been at war with Judah for many years. For this reason, they did not like the Judeans. Once again, pride entered in—pride for their country. While true patriotism can be good, when we allow pride to take over, then nationalism takes over; and this can become destructive. We begin to think that we are better than others; thus, we reason, we have a right to defend our honor and to hurt others if needed. Nationalism can take on many forms. We can be overly proud of our country, state or city, of our family, of our school or of an athletic team. When someone says or does something that appears threatening to these things, we become angry and "come to their rescue." When we have this kind of attitude, Satan will use it to create problems for us and for others.

A fourth reason for their anger was probably *disgust*. These soldiers had made a long trip to Judah for nothing. They had come prepared for battle and now had to cart everything back home. No doubt they were annoyed and disgusted at the inconvenience. Instead of becoming angry, however, they should have seen what a blessing had been given to them by bringing them to Judah. They should have been thankful that they could be in a country where the people worshiped the true God. If these soldiers had really been smart, they would have wanted to stay and serve the Lord. But their selfishness and pride kept them from seeing this.

Isn't it amazing—and tragic—how we can become angry over the smallest matters? The slightest hurt or injustice, the simplest selfish desire, the smallest inconvenience will often send us into a fit of rage. Stop and evaluate your own anger. How many times have one of these causes—pride, selfishness, nationalism or disgust—been at the root? The first step in overcoming anger is to identify the object of our anger and the reasons behind it. Then we need to admit that we are foolish for becoming angry for no valid reason and make an effort to dispel these angry thoughts—before they cause problems.

The Consequences of Their Anger

Unjustified anger almost always has grave consequences—both for us and for others. What were the consequences of this army's anger? Second Chronicles 25:13 tells us, "But the soldiers of the army which Amaziah sent back, that they should not go with him to battle, fell upon the cities of Judah, from Samaria even unto Beth-horon, and smote three thousand of them, and took much spoil." Amaziah and his army had gone to fight the Edomites, leaving the villages in Judah unprotected. Since they couldn't punish Amaziah, the Israelite soldiers instead vented their anger on the innocent people of Judah. They ravaged the villages and took whatever they wanted, killing 3000 men, women and children in the process.

After soundly defeating the Edomites, Amaziah and his army returned to find the destruction left by the Israelite army. The king was enraged, and no doubt embarrassed, by what the Israelite soldiers had done. Once again pride and nationalism entered in. Amaziah, who was feeling proud and strong after his victory, decided to go to war with Israel in order to avenge his country's loss (see vv. 17-19).

Once the cycle of anger starts, it is hard to stop. Seeking revenge only leads to retaliation from the other side. Soon the anger is out of control. And when this happens, innocent people are almost always caught in the crossfire. If we cannot vent our anger on those who caused our rage, we frequently vent it on others—usually on anyone in our path. This is what the Israelite army did. Since they couldn't punish Amaziah, they took out their anger on the people instead.

In Amaziah, we see the danger of anger that is motivated by sin and pride. Even after the Lord corrected Amaziah for his faithlessness in hiring the Israelite army, he continued to ignore the Lord. God gave the king a great victory in Edom, and how did he repay Him? By replacing the Lord with idols from the country he had just conquered: "Now it came to pass, after that Amaziah was come from the slaughter of the Edomites, that he brought the gods of the children of Seir [Edom], and set them up to be his gods, and bowed down himself before them, and burned incense unto them. Wherefore the anger of the Lord was kindled against Amaziah" (vv. 14,15). God sent a prophet to Amaziah to confront him with his sin and to pronounce judgment on him (see vv. 15,16). But once again Amaziah allowed anger to blind him to his sin. Instead of confessing his guilt, Amaziah became angry at the prophet and at God.

Anger blinded Amaziah to his sin. And pride blinded him to the consequences of his anger. The prophet told Amaziah, "I know that God hath determined to destroy thee, because thou hast not hearkened unto my counsel" (v. 16). But Amaziah became proud. He thought he could win the battle without the Lord's help. So he ignored the prophet's warning and challenged Joash, the king of Israel, to meet him on the battlefield. Even Joash tried to warn Amaziah, saying, "Thou sayest, Lo, thou hast smitten the Edomites; and thine heart lifteth thee up to boast: abide now at home; why shouldest thou meddle to thine hurt, that thou shouldest fall, even thou, and Judah with thee?" (v. 19). But Joash's warning only served to anger Amaziah even further. He went up against Joash and his army and was soundly defeated on the battlefield. And, once again, innocent men were killed in the process.

When we use anger and pride as a cover for sin, it always leads to problems. Proverbs 16:18 tells us, "Pride goeth before destruction, and an haughty spirit before a fall." Proverbs 18:12 adds, "Before destruction the heart of man is haughty, and before honour is humility." If Amaziah had only humbled himself and confessed his sins to God instead of becoming angry, he could have saved himself and the nation much heartache. But he became his own worst enemy. Joash and his army broke down the walls of Jerusalem and took the gold, the silver and the holy vessels from the temple; they also took Amaziah's treasures (see II Chron. 25:21-24). Amaziah was not killed in the battle; however, his sin continued to haunt him. He was later assassinated by his own people (see vv. 27,28). Amaziah lost his wealth, his honor and eventually his life because of his pride, selfishness and anger.

Anger is like a small hole in a dike. It doesn't appear to be much of a problem at first. However, if the hole is not plugged quickly, the water will gradually enlarge the hole until the dam breaks and we are faced with a raging flood. This is why Proverbs 17:14 warns us, "The beginning of strife is as when one letteth out water: therefore leave off contention, before it be meddled with."

When we become angry, we must resolve it immediately. Anger that continues to burn within us soon becomes an uncontrollable fire that destroys us and those we love. Proverbs 26:21 states, "As coals are to burning coals, and wood to fire; so is a contentious man to kindle strife." When we become angry, we add fuel to the fire. What otherwise might have been a minor problem soon grows beyond control when sparked by anger.

The key to dealing with anger is self-control, which only the Holy Spirit can produce in us. When anger arises, we must take an honest look at ourselves to determine the source of that anger. If it is the result of pride, selfishness or some other sin, we should humbly confess it to God. He will then fill us with the love that we need to control the anger within us.

Chapter 9

An Angry Congregation

Have you ever been angry at a preacher? Were you ever in a congregation that was so angry it stood up en masse, escorted the preacher out, and then tried to kill him? While it is unlikely that any congregation in the United States would physically harm their minister, believers do become angry at the pastor and other church members and frequently attack them verbally. However, some missionaries in other countries are abused or even killed by the people they have come to serve.

The Bible speaks of a number of prophets and preachers who gave their lives proclaiming God's message of salvation. Stephen is just one example. His sermon, recorded in Acts 7, so angered those listening that they immediately took him out and stoned him (see vv. 54-60).

Likewise, the greatest minister who ever preached also suffered this kind of abuse. What is even more ironic is the fact that He was in His hometown preaching among His friends and neighbors. That man, of course, was Jesus Christ. In Luke 4 we read: "And all they in the synagogue, when they heard these things, were filled with wrath, and rose up, and thrust him out of the city, and led him unto the brow of the hill whereon their city was built, that they might cast him down headlong. But he passing through the midst of them went his way" (vv. 28-30).

What would cause Christ's friends and neighbors to turn against Him that way? What did He say that made them so angry? And why do Christians today become angry at fellow believers? Let's attend that synagogue service in Nazareth and watch the congregation as it moves from one experience to another. By discovering the dynamic at work in this situation, we can learn some of the causes of anger in the Body of Christ today and find ways to deal with this anger.

They Were Assembled

In Luke 4:16 we see the congregation in Nazareth assembled in the synagogue for their weekly time of prayer and instruction. However, this would be no ordinary service, for Jesus had decided to join them: "And he came to Nazareth, where he had been brought up: and, as his custom was, he went into the synagogue on the sabbath day, and stood up for to read."

The synagogue was very important to the spiritual life of the Jewish people in Christ's day. The word "synagogue" means "gathering together." In the Old Testament, the tabernacle—and later the temple—was the primary place of worship. But then the Children of Israel were taken into captivity and scattered throughout Asia Minor. Because they could no longer come to the temple regularly to worship and offer sacrifices, they developed local synagogues where they could meet for the reading and expounding of the Scriptures and for prayer. The purpose of the synagogue was not so much worship as it was instruction. Unlike the temple, all the people could enter the synagogue, however only the men could participate in the service. Children were permitted to come to the synagogue from the age of five or six and were required to attend the services once they reached the age of 16.

While the intent and purpose of the synagogue had been good in the beginning, by the time of Christ we find that the Jewish religion had decayed tremendously. The Pharisees and other religious leaders had added so many interpretations to the Law that it had become a religion of works rather than true worship. So many rules and regulations existed that the people couldn't possibly have obeyed them all. Many people went to the synagogue out of a sense of obligation rather than from a real desire to learn and to worship.

Yet we find Jesus attending the synagogue services regularly. We can think of many reasons why He could have chosen *not* to meet with God's people. He certainly had no need for learning. The people were sinful and rebellious. The synagogue services lacked real meaning and worship. Christ had come to show the people a better way and to lead them back to God. To us, it would have seemed more logical for Jesus to reject the institutions and practices of the day and to work apart from the local congregations. However, He often chose to work in the synagogue, despite its flaws and problems.

How often have you heard people say, "The church is full of hypocrites and sinners. The sermons and classes are boring. Besides, I don't need to go to church. I can worship God just as well at home, maybe better"? However, God's Word tells us, "Let us consider one another to provoke unto love and to good works: not forsaking the assembling of ourselves together, as the manner of some is; but exhorting one another: and so much the more, as ye see the day approaching" (Heb. 10:24,25). Not only has the Lord commanded Christians to meet together regularly, but He also set the example for us. Despite its flaws and problems, we need the fellowship and worship that the local church provides.

They Were Attentive

For whatever reasons the people had chosen to assemble in the synagogue that Sabbath, once Jesus stood up and began to read, the congregation immediately became attentive. We find this same kind of response wherever Jesus went. He always spoke with such authority and power that the people couldn't help but listen.

In Luke 4 we find the people's attention focused on two things. First, we see that they were *attentive to the reading of God's Word*. "And there was delivered unto him the book of the prophet Esaias [Isaiah]. And when he had opened the book, he found the place where it was written, 'The Spirit of the Lord is upon me, because he hath anointed me to preach the gospel to the poor; he hath sent me to heal the brokenhearted, to preach deliverance to the captives, and recovering of sight to the blind, to set at liberty them that are bruised, to preach the acceptable year of the Lord' " (vv. 17-19). Before delivering His message to the people, Jesus began by reading from Isaiah 61.

Christ's example here shows us the importance of reading God's Word in public. In I Timothy 4:13 we are told, "Give attendance to reading," which literally means "be devoted to the public reading of the Word of God." When the early believers broke away from the synagogue, they took this practice with them. The public reading of the Scriptures was a part of every service in the early church.

Unfortunately, many evangelical churches today have abandoned this practice. I'm amazed at how many people who claim to defend and to preach the Word of God do not encourage the public reading of the Scriptures. Often the sermon text is the only passage that is read during a service. We need to have a balanced reading of the Old Testament, the Gospels and the Epistles.

It was said of Dr. G. Campbell Morgan, the great British expositor, that people learned more from his public reading of the Scriptures than they did from the sermons of other preachers. Why was this true? First, and foremost, was the fact that he was reading God's Word. The Scriptures have the power to transform lives. God's Word never returns to Him void (see Isa. 55:11). However, Dr. Morgan was especially successful because he carefully prepared for his public readings of the Word. Before he stood to read, he always studied the passage thoroughly. Many churches do not see results from their Bible readings because they don't have this kind of preparation. I have attended services where someone has been asked at the last minute to stand and read the Word of God. This is wrong. Before God's Word is read in any worship service, the readers should have prepared their hearts and minds through personal study of the passage and prayer so that they are able to read it with meaning and with power.

Not only should we be faithful in the public reading of God's Word, but this incident in the life of Christ also shows us the importance of being *attentive to the preaching of the Word.* When Jesus had finished reading from the Book of Isaiah, "he closed the book, and he gave it again to the minister, and sat down. And the eyes of all them that were in the synagogue were fastened on him. And he began to say unto them, This day is this scripture fulfilled in your ears" (Luke 4:20,21). Jesus then proceeded to teach them the meaning of Isaiah's prophecy.

In stating that He was the fulfillment of this prophecy, Jesus was claiming a great deal. The Greek word for "sent" in verse 18 is *apostello*, a word meaning "to be sent forth on a mission." It was used to refer to those who had received a special commission from God Himself. From this word we get the word apostle. This particular passage in Isaiah 61 was a messianic prophecy. Thus, Jesus

113

was boldly proclaiming, "I am the Messiah." In fact, verse 18 is a revelation of the Trinity: "The Spirit [Holy Spirit] of the Lord [the Father] is upon me [the Son]."

Furthermore, Christ said He had come "to preach the acceptable year of the Lord" (Luke 4:19). This was a direct reference to the Year of Jubilee. When God gave the Law to the Israelites, He had set aside every 50th year as a year of rest and restoration (see Lev. 25). There was to be no sowing or reaping that year so the soil could rest. Also, property that had been sold to pay a debt was to be returned to the original owner or his heirs. Likewise, those who had sold themselves into slavery to pay a debt were to be released. Many celebrations were held during this time. The Year of Jubilee was a year of redemption and rejoicing. Thus, Jesus was saying, in effect, "I am proclaiming a spiritual Year of Jubilee. I have come to bring redemption and rejoicing."

In Isaiah's prophecy, we find five groups of people who are helped by the coming of the Messiah. In each we discover both a literal and a spiritual fulfillment. First, Jesus said that the Spirit of the Lord had anointed Him to "preach the gospel to the poor" (Luke 4:18). Unlike many of the religious leaders of His day, Jesus frequently ministered to the poor in Palestine. He provided for their physical needs on several occasions. But even more importantly, Jesus came to help the poor in spirit. Who is poorer than a lost sinner? No one is rich enough to purchase his redemption. Only Christ can save us.

Likewise, Jesus said He came to heal the brokenhearted and to give sight to the blind (v. 18). Of course, He did heal many people of blindness and other illnesses and often gave words of encouragement to the lonely and depressed. But greater still is the spiritual healing that we receive when we give Him all the pieces of our broken hearts and lives. He came to help the spiritually blind—to open their eyes to the truth of God's Word.

Finally, Jesus added that He had come to "preach deliverance to the captives, . . . to set at liberty them that are bruised" (v. 18). During His ministry Jesus freed many people from sickness and death. Later, we find Him miraculously releasing the apostles from prison on several occasions. But He provided an even greater freedom for us when He released us from the bondage of Satan.

What a message of hope Christ has given us! He offers freedom and help to everyone, no matter how bankrupt, brokenhearted, bound, blind or bruised they may be. The good news of the Gospel is that we don't have to stay the way we are. Jesus Christ can transform our lives when we give ourselves to Him.

They Were Astonished

As Jesus spoke to the people, they listened attentively. However, their reaction reveals that His message had not changed their hearts and minds: "And all bare him witness, and wondered at the gracious words which proceeded out of his mouth. And they said, Is not this Joseph's son?" (Luke

115

4:22). The people were astonished at what Jesus told them; however, not in the way that we might imagine. They were shocked and surprised that He would make such claims about Himself. They did not believe that He was really the Messiah.

Why did they have so much trouble accepting what Jesus told them? Because they thought they knew Him when they really didn't. After all, they reasoned, Jesus had grown up among them in Nazareth. They knew He was the foster son of Joseph the carpenter and that He Himself was a skilled carpenter. Even though they had probably recognized that there was something different about this young man, they could never pinpoint exactly what it was. However, even when Jesus told them what made Him so special, they refused to believe it. Christ simply didn't fit their conception of God's promised Messiah.

The people were astonished not only at what Jesus claimed to be but also at what He claimed they were. They told Him, in effect, "What does this have to do with us? Do we look blind or bruised? Are we being held captive? We certainly aren't poor and destitute. Why do we need You? We have the religion of our fathers." Because they could not accept who Jesus was and could not see their own spiritual need, the people did not apply God's Word to themselves.

They Were Alarmed

However, the people could not escape or explain away the meaning of Christ's following words to

116

them. The point was all too clear. "And he said unto them, Ye will surely say unto me this proverb, Physician, heal thyself: whatsoever we have heard done in Capernaum, do also here in thy country. And he said, Verily I say unto you, No prophet is accepted in his own country. But I tell you of a truth, many widows were in Israel in the days of Elias [Elijah], when the heaven was shut up three years and six months, when great famine was throughout all the land; but unto none of them was Elias sent, save unto Sarepta, a city of Sidon, unto a woman that was a widow. And many lepers were in Israel in the time of Eliseus [Elisha] the prophet; and none of them was cleansed, saving Naaman the Syrian" (Luke 4:23-27).

When the people heard this, they became alarmed. Why? Because they realized that Jesus was no ordinary rabbi. Other teachers would simply reiterate what those before them had said. They would exalt Israel's past or talk about its great future. But Jesus spoke with power and authority. And He knew exactly what the people were thinking and feeling. He *exposed their unbelief.* Jesus told them, in effect, "I know what you are thinking. You're saying to yourself, *If You really are the Messiah, then show us what You can do. Perform a miracle, and then we will believe You.* However, miracles alone will never change your hearts. I know you won't accept Me. A prophet is never accepted in his own country."

Jesus then *exposed their pride.* He reached back into Jewish history and gave them two examples of

117

prophets who had ministered to people whom the Jews had rejected (see vv. 25-27). And when we examine these examples closely, we can understand the full impact of what Jesus was saying to these people. Note the people that were helped by Elijah and Elisha. The widow of Sarepta was a Sidonian. Naaman was a Syrian. Neither one was a Jew or even a proselyte.

This becomes significant when we remember how the Jews felt about themselves and about the Gentiles. They took great pride in the fact that they were God's chosen people. Likewise, they looked down on anyone who was not a Jew. It was inconceivable to them that God would do something for the Gentiles. And here was Jesus, reminding these Jews in Nazareth of the fact that God had not only helped two Gentiles but had given them something that the Jews themselves had rejected. The meaning was all too clear. Jesus was saying to them, "If you continue to reject Me, I will offer God's grace and salvation to the Gentiles."

Nothing smashes the pride of sinful man like the sovereignty of God. God has *chosen* to save us. Without His grace and mercy, we would be hopelessly lost. Jonah stated it perfectly when he said, "Salvation is of the Lord" (Jon. 2:9). When we are tempted to become proud of our position and to look down on the unsaved, we need to remember that we have done nothing to merit our salvation. We are saved only because we have placed our faith in Jesus Christ. This realization should humble us and cause us to love and honor our Saviour even more.

They Were Angry

Christ's words struck at the heart of the Jews' pride and unbelief. Suddenly, they saw themselves as they really were. And, as often happens when our sin is exposed to us, the congregation became defensive and angry. Luke 4:28,29 states, "And all they in the synagogue, when they heard these things, were filled with wrath, and rose up, and thrust him out of the city, and led him unto the brow of the hill whereon their city was built, that they might cast him down headlong." The congregation was so enraged that the members dragged Jesus outside the city and tried to kill Him.

Why were they so angry? I think that St. Augustine said it perfectly in his confessions: "They love truth when it enlightens them. They hate truth when it accuses them. They love truth when it reveals itself and hate it when it reveals them." If Jesus had given this Jewish congregation a lovely devotional sermon about the brokenhearted and about the ministry of the coming Messiah, they would have welcomed Him with open arms. However, Jesus did not preach this kind of sermon. He took the Word of God and applied it directly to their hearts, convicting them of their sin. And these people did not want to have their hearts and lives exposed in this way. They wanted soothing promises, not burning convictions. Why? Because they were proud and refused to yield to God.

Christians today need to be convicted. However, some pastors are often afraid to preach convicting sermons. They don't want to anger their members. However, I would much rather have people become angry at my message than to be so complacent that they did not hear a word I said.

How do you listen to a sermon? When you hear it, do you immediately apply it to the person next to you, saying, "Preach on, Pastor! My wife needs to hear that"? Or do you listen carefully and quietly, allowing the Lord to speak to you? The writer James has given us the formula for controlling our anger when we are under conviction. He stated, "Let every man be swift to hear, slow to speak, slow to wrath: for the wrath of man worketh not the righteousness of God" (James 1:19,20). We need to listen with open hearts and minds, yielding our wills to the power and truth of God's Word.

Jesus is the Great Physician (see Luke 4:23). And like any physician, before the Lord can heal a person, He must first diagnose the illness and prescribe the proper treatment. However, we must accept the diagnosis and treatment before healing can take place. And the treatment frequently is painful. Often He must wound us before He can heal us. But the pain He asks us to endure is minute compared to the wounds He suffered on the cross in our behalf (see Isa. 53:4,5).

The congregation at Nazareth was not willing to accept the Lord's diagnosis. Instead of becoming angry at their sin, their exclusiveness, their jealousy, their pride and their nationalism, they became

120

angry at God. As a result, they resisted the work of God and rejected the Son of God. Let's not make the same mistake. Allow God's Word to expose the sin and rebellion in your heart. Willingly accept His correction, and He will heal you.

Chapter 10

An Angry Ruler

While anger is a problem for every person, it is even more serious when a leader is involved. Why? Because anger is not the best way to accomplish God's work. James 1:20 tells us, "The wrath of man worketh not the righteousness of God." When the spiritual leaders are angry, the work of the church suffers. The Apostle Paul realized this. That is why he instructed the believers to choose men for the office of bishop who were "not soon angry" (Titus 1:7). While Paul was referring primarily to elders, pastors and other church leaders, this requirement applies to any kind of leader. Because leaders are responsible for the lives and well-being of other people, it is vital that they learn how to exercise self-control.

In Luke 13 we read about a Jewish religious leader, the ruler of a synagogue, who had a serious problem with anger. When he became angry with Jesus, he did not deal with his anger properly. Rather than coming to Jesus, he took out his anger on the congregation. Luke 13:10-17 tells us, "And he [Jesus] was teaching in one of the synagogues on the sabbath. And, behold, there was a woman which had a spirit of infirmity eighteen years, and was bowed together, and could in no wise lift up herself. And when Jesus saw her, he called her to him, and said unto her, Woman, thou art loosed from thine infirmity. And he laid his hands on her: and immediately she was made straight, and glorified God. And the ruler of the synagogue answered with indignation, because that Jesus had healed on the sabbath day, and said unto the people, There are six days in which men ought to work: in them therefore come and be healed, and not on the sabbath day.

"The Lord then answered him, and said, Thou hypocrite, doth not each one of you on the sabbath loose his ox or his ass from the stall, and lead him away to watering? And ought not this woman, being a daughter of Abraham, whom Satan hath bound, lo, these eighteen years, be loosed from this bond on the sabbath day? And when he had said these things, all his adversaries were ashamed: and all the people rejoiced for all the glorious things that were done by him."

In order to properly understand this incident and the ruler's anger, we must first see this ruler in the light of the culture of that day. The ruler of the synagogue was not what we would consider to be a pastor. He was not the spiritual leader of the people. He was in charge of the public services in the synagogue. He was responsible for choosing people to read the Scriptures and to lead the people in prayer. He supervised the care of the building. It was his duty to see that the services started on time and that they were not interrupted, making sure that everything was done decently and in order.

Thus, when Jesus interrupted the service to heal this woman, the ruler did not stop to consider the woman and her needs. He was only concerned about holding an orderly service, but Jesus had excited the people and upset this order. Even worse was the fact that this Teacher had broken the Jewish law that forbade people to work on the Sabbath. So, in an effort to restore his own position of authority, the ruler became angry, scolding the people for breaking this Sabbath law.

The ruler's response teaches us an important truth about anger: *Anger is often a sign of deficiencies in our life.* Frequently we use anger to hide the fact that we are lacking important inner qualities. As we look at this ruler, we see that he was using anger to cover up at least four deficiencies in his life— qualities that are vital for a close walk with the Lord.

He Lacked Discernment

The ruler's first deficiency was a lack of discernment. He was unable to discern between good and evil. He could not see that *God was in the synagogue!* The ruler did not recognize who Jesus really was—God in the flesh.

When we examine the Scriptures closely, we discover that this was probably the last time Jesus taught publicly in the synagogue. At least it is the last record we have of His synagogue ministry. This incident took place just a few months before our Lord's crucifixion.

Imagine having the privilege of hearing Jesus teach in person—to be able to hear the Word from

124

the Living Word Himself! This ruler had that opportunity, but he did not take advantage of it. How do we know this? Because if he had really been listening to what Jesus said and had applied the Word to his life, he would not have responded as he did when the Lord healed the woman. If he had really taken God's Word to heart, it would have made him a better person, for the Word of God is light (Ps. 119:105). It shines into our hearts and dispels the darkness. The Word of God is food (Matt. 4:4; Heb. 5:12-14; I Pet. 2:2). It comes into our souls and gives us nourishment. The Word of God is water (Eph. 5:26). It washes and cleanses our mind and our heart. The Word of God is seed (Luke 8:11). When it is planted and nurtured, it produces the fruit of the Spirit in us (Gal. 5:22,23). However, the ruler did not receive any of these benefits because the Word never entered his heart. He was too busy with his responsibilities to recognize the fact that Jesus was no ordinary teacher. God was in his synagogue, and he didn't even notice.

Likewise, because this ruler lacked spiritual discernment, he could not see that *Satan was also in the synagogue.* His influence was felt in the crippled woman. Since the Lord Jesus did not cast a demon out of the woman, we can assume that she was not demon possessed. However, the Scriptures do describe her as having "a spirit of infirmity" (Luke 13:11). Likewise, Jesus stated that the woman had been bound by Satan (see v. 16). This gives us the impression that Satan had somehow used a demonic force to cause this physical affliction. And because her illness was controlled by Satan, no one had been able to heal her. She couldn't raise herself up, and nobody else could help her either.

As I read this passage in Luke, I get the impression that this woman was not present when Jesus began teaching but that she arrived later. Coming in late to a service is embarrassing under normal conditions. And when we consider this woman's physical problems and the seating arrangement of the synagogue, her embarrassment was no doubt even more acute. Seating in the synagogue was carefully arranged, with the men on one side of the room and the women on the other. She probably sat at the back of the room. Even more attention would have been drawn to her because of her handicap. Her illness had left her so crippled that she could no longer stand up straight. She was completely bent over, so she no doubt had a difficult time walking or even seeing where she was going. Her entrance into the synagogue more than likely elicited stares and hushed comments from the congregation.

How do you react when someone comes in late to a service, especially a person who looks or acts odd? If you are like most people, you are irritated by the interruption. I imagine that this was the ruler's reaction. No doubt he saw this woman as she hobbled in, and he was probably exasperated at her for drawing attention to herself in this way. He probably thought to himself, *What is that woman doing here? Why can't she be on time like the rest of us!*

Jesus also would have seen this woman as she

entered the room. Yet we do not find Him resenting her interruption. Rather, He showed her compassion and kindness. He knew the hold that Satan had on her life, and He took immediate steps to release her from this oppression.

We can only imagine the suffering and pain that this woman had endured for 18 long years. It would have been easy for her to become bitter and angry toward God for not answering her prayers for healing. Yet it doesn't appear that this woman did that. Despite the supreme effort it took for her to go anywhere, she came to the synagogue on the Sabbath to worship God. The passage gives no indication that the women knew beforehand that Jesus would be in the synagogue or that she thought He could heal her. She did not come to Him and beg to be healed. Jesus spoke to her first, calling her to come to Him. He then laid His hands on her and healed her (see vv. 12,13). Her prayers had been answered at last!

The ruler of the synagogue had the rare privilege of seeing and hearing God in the flesh. He had listened to the Word being taught as it had never been taught before. A miracle had been performed before his very eyes. Yet, instead of using this opportunity to glorify God, he became angry. Why? Because he lacked discernment.

He Lacked Power

The ruler's anger also revealed a lack of power in his life. He resented the fact that Jesus had usurped his authority in the synagogue. He was jealous of the power that the Lord displayed. He had been conducting the synagogue services for years. He had obeyed the Law and the Jewish rituals to the letter. Yet his spiritual life was dead. He knew that he did not have this kind of power; therefore, he felt threatened by Jesus. So he fought off this attack to his pride and authority in the only way he knew how—by becoming angry.

When you read the ruler's response carefully, you realize just how senseless and absurd his comment really was. He told the people, "There are six days in which men ought to work: in them therefore come and be healed, and not on the sabbath day" (Luke 13:14). But who would perform the healing? Was he going to do it? He couldn't be sure that Jesus would be there each time a person came to the synagogue to be healed.

Anger frequently leads us to say things that we later regret. A quick temper reveals to everyone just how weak we really are. When the ruler saw the power that Jesus possessed, he should have willingly admitted, "I have no power. The Law has no power. Our Jewish traditions and rituals are powerless. Only Jesus can save you and heal you." However, he did not say this. Instead, he became angry, thinking that it would be a sign of his strength and authority. But it only showed the people how powerless and weak-willed he really was.

Like the ruler, so many religious groups today are "holding to a form of godliness, although they have denied its power" (II Tim. 3:5, NASB). They are so concerned about their traditions and programs that

128

they have no time for helping people. Likewise, we find few false religions running rescue missions or rehabilitation centers. Why? Because they have no message for lost sinners. They are powerless to help them. Instead of turning to the Lord, these groups continue to rely on their man-made traditions and false teachings, leading many people astray in the process.

Even though Jesus healed this woman publicly as an example to everyone present, He did not treat her merely as an instrument to be used for His display of power. He saw her as an individual—not just as one of the crowd. He looked deep within her and saw the burden in her heart. He felt her need. He called to her and told her to come to Him. Then He gently touched her and loosed her from her infirmity.

That word "loosed" is very important in this passage. In verse 15 Jesus said that these people would loose their ox or their ass and take them to water them. In verse 16 He said, "Shouldn't this woman, who's a child of Abraham, made in the image of God, be loosed from this Satanic bondage?" The same word is used in both verses. Jesus clearly pointed out the ruler's lack of compassion. He would treat an animal better than he would treat this woman.

Why did Jesus choose to expose this woman's need publicly? Instead of making her walk all the way to the front where everyone could see her, He could have gone to her after the service and quietly healed her. This would have seemed like a more logical choice, especially when we consider the fact that He was aware of the Jewish law forbidding any kind of work on the Sabbath. However, Jesus did not try to hide His power or His work. One reason why we do not see this kind of power in the Church today may be that few Christians are willing to be open and honest about their faith. If more believers would simply do what Jesus wants them to do— without worrying about the possible consequences— great things could happen.

He Lacked Freedom

The ruler's anger revealed not only his lack of discernment and of power but also his lack of freedom. If you had asked this man, "Are you free?" he would have quickly replied, "Of course I am. I am a Jew, a son of Abraham. We are God's chosen people. We Jews have never been in bondage to anyone."

This was the prevailing attitude among the Jews of that day. They were extremely proud of their heritage and of the fact that they were God's chosen people. It seems strange, however, that they would even make such a statement when you consider their history. They had been ruled by various nations for hundreds of years. In the Book of Judges you find the Israelites under bondage to six different nations. Later, they were carried away into captivity by Babylon. This was followed by bondage to the Medo-Persians and the Greeks. And even at this time in history, they were under Roman domination and rule. But whenever the Lord confronted the Jews about their lack of freedom, they would hotly retort, "We be Abraham's seed, and were never in bondage to any man: how sayest thou, Ye shall be made free?" (John 8:33).

However, what these Jews didn't understand was that Jesus was not referring to physical bondage but rather to spiritual slavery. While the crippled woman was in physical bondage, the ruler of the synagogue was in a far worse state, for he was in spiritual bondage. Satan had so bound him with traditions and laws that he could not even worship God freely. The Jews had added so many traditions to the Sabbath observance that the Sabbath had become a burden instead of a blessing. God had originally instituted the Sabbath as simply a day of physical rest for both people and animals. But then the Jews began to add stipulations to God's simple law. For example, the people were only allowed to walk a certain number of feet on the Sabbath. They had dozens of rules forbidding certain kinds of work on the Sabbath. If a person got a sliver in his finger, he could have been punished for carrying a burden on the Sabbath. If he had removed it, he would have broken one of the laws against working. The Jews spent so much time worrying about breaking a law, or looking for ways to get around the laws, that they had little time for rest on the Sabbath.

The ruler of the synagogue was so concerned about these Jewish traditions that he wound up defending the Sabbath rather than the God of the Sabbath. He had forgotten the Lord's beautiful instructions to him in Micah 6:8: "He hath shewed

131

thee, O man, what is good; and what doth the Lord require of thee, but to do justly, and to love mercy, and to walk humbly with thy God?" The ruler was certainly not being very just, merciful or humble. When he saw the woman come in, he should have said, "Welcome, my friend. I see you have a great need. Why don't we all pause and ask Jehovah God to help you." But he did not love God from his heart. Therefore, he was only concerned about maintaining his man-made traditions. He was also afraid of the people and of their reaction to Jesus. He was afraid of breaking out of the mold he was in. This ruler was in bondage to the Law, to tradition and to fear. His anger revealed his lack of freedom.

He Lacked Honesty

Finally, the ruler's anger revealed his lack of honesty. When the ruler scolded the people for coming to be healed on the Sabbath, Jesus called him a hypocrite (see Luke 13:15). In some texts the word "hypocrite" is plural. No doubt the ruler of the synagogue was not the only Jew present who bristled when the Lord healed this woman. Some probably looked at each other and said, "This man can't be from God. He wouldn't violate the Sabbath if He were truly a prophet of God." In fact, the passage indicates that more than one person opposed Jesus. After the Lord had powerfully defended the woman and His actions, the Bible tells us, "All his adversaries were ashamed" (v. 17).

Why did Jesus call the ruler a hypocrite? Because He knew that the man was only feigning spirituality

132

and devotion to God. A hypocrite is someone who deliberately deceives. The word comes from a Greek word that refers to a play actor or one who assumes a role. During the time of Christ, Greek actors would wear masks during a play. Each mask represented a different character. Each time the actor changed his mask, the audience knew that a new character was speaking.

What an apt description of the ruler! Whenever he came into the synagogue, he put on his mask of spirituality and enforced the Law to the letter. However, outside the synagogue, he did as he pleased. But he could not hide his deception from Jesus. The Lord knew exactly what kind of person he was. He told the ruler, in effect, "You hypocrite! You will break the Sabbath laws at home in order to care for your animals, yet you refuse to bend the rules even a little in order to help a person in need. You pretend to defend the Law while you continually break it yourself!" (see vv. 15,16). The ruler's anger was hypocritical and dishonest. He was not concerned about defending God or helping others; he was only concerned about himself and about defending his position of authority.

Not only was the ruler dishonest in his anger, but he was cowardly as well. In reality, the ruler was angry at Jesus—not at the people. He wanted to attack the Lord Jesus, but he was afraid to confront Him. So he lashed out at the people instead, saying, "There are six days in which men ought to work: in them therefore come and be healed" (v. 14). But he really was talking to Jesus, and the Lord knew it.

133

Likewise, the ruler's anger revealed his unwillingness to love and to praise the Lord. Jesus had just performed a great miracle. The woman was standing before them completely healed. The congregation should have stood and joined her in singing praises to God. But, instead, the ruler and others became critical of Jesus for interrupting the service and for breaking their precious rules. But the Lord saw through their hypocrisy and exposed them for what they really were. "And when he had said these things, all his adversaries were ashamed: and all the people rejoiced for all the glorious things that were done by him" (v. 17).

While we should defend what we think is right, we must do so in love, humility and kindness. Before we become angry at someone, we need to examine the reasons for our anger closely to make sure that we are not merely hiding our own deficiencies. We need to ask the Lord for the discernment to know when we should become angry and when we should not. We must be honest about our angry feelings and be willing to admit when we are wrong. We need to remember the freedom that we have in Christ and not try to enslave people with our interpretations of Scripture. And, most of all, we need to submit ourselves to the Lord and allow His power to flow through us, for only His power is strong enough to control the rage within us.

Chapter 11

An Angry Brother

The only thing worse than a child trying to act like an adult is an adult acting childish. And nothing makes a person look more childish than selfish anger. If we are thinking only of ourselves, we will become angry and resentful whenever we do not get what we want. Jesus once told a parable about a man who became angry at his father because of the attention his brother was receiving. That man, of course, was the elder brother in the story of the Prodigal Son (see Luke 15:11-32).

In studying this parable, we tend to focus our attention on the son who left home rather than on the one who stayed. However, if you read this passage in the context of the beginning of the chapter, you discover that Jesus may have been teaching something far more than what we have generally understood. Notice the response of the elder brother when his father throws a lavish celebration to welcome home his wayward son: "Now his elder son was in the field: and as he came and drew nigh to the house, he heard musick and dancing. And he called one of the servants, and asked what these things meant. And he said unto him, Thy brother is

135

come; and thy father hath killed the fatted calf, because he hath received him safe and sound. And he was angry, and would not go in: therefore came his father out, and intreated him. And he answering said to his father, Lo, these many years do I serve thee, neither transgressed I at any time thy commandment: and yet thou never gavest me a kid, that I might make merry with my friends: but as soon as this thy son was come, which hath devoured thy living with harlots, thou hast killed for him the fatted calf. And he said unto him, Son, thou art ever with me, and all that I have is thine. It was meet that we should make merry, and be glad: for this thy brother was dead, and is alive again; and was lost, and is found" (vv. 25-32).

Unfortunately, we don't know how this story ends. Like so many other incidents in the Bible, God does not give us all the details. He leaves it open so we can draw our own conclusions. In doing so, we frequently discover what is in our own heart. We can only hope that the elder son repented and asked for his father's forgiveness and then joined the family wholeheartedly in welcoming his brother home.

But the key to understanding the meaning of this parable lies in the beginning of this passage rather than the end. The opening verses of Luke 15 reveal Christ's purpose for telling this story: "Then drew near unto him all the publicans [tax collectors] and sinners for to hear him. And the Pharisees and scribes murmured, saying, This man receiveth sinners, and eateth with them" (vv. 1,2). In this parable Jesus was addressing two groups of people. The Prodigal Son represented the tax collectors and sinners, while the elder brother was an illustration of the Pharisees and the scribes. And, as we will see, Jesus had a pointed message for each.

When we look at the life of the elder brother, we discover many aspects of his life that were quite commendable. He certainly was a faithful, hard-working man. He had high morals and never disgraced his father's name. However, he was an outsider. He had remained outside the fellowship of his family. He didn't recognize—and therefore didn't enjoy—the liberty and blessings that were his as a member of the family. The scribes and Pharisees had this same problem. Because they were religious people who upheld God's Law to the letter, they thought they were inside the family of God. However, they had never trusted Christ as their Saviour. Thus, they remained outside of the family and missed the blessings they could have enjoyed.

How do you respond to the spiritual victories of others? Do you genuinely rejoice with them, or do you become angry and jealous at the blessings they receive? Your response is often an indication of where you are in the fellowship of the Body. Becoming angry at the victories of others may mean that your relationship with the Lord isn't what it should be.

Why Is He Outside?

In order to understand the elder brother's anger—and our own—we must first attempt to answer

137

some rather pointed questions. First, why did the elder brother remain outside instead of joining the rest of the household at the party? Because he was angry. However, in order to fully understand the reasons for his anger, we need to look at those with whom he was angry. First, we see that *he was angry at his father.*

This anger was probably motivated by several factors. First was the fact that his father had *forgiven* his younger brother. As the bedraggled, unwashed boy drew near the village, his father ran out to meet him. He threw his arms around his son, hugging and kissing him. Nothing was said about what the boy had done. Instead of punishing him, the father treated his wayward son like a king. This enraged the older son. He wanted to see his younger brother punished. Why? Because he was not willing to forgive him.

No doubt we are moved by this scene each time we read it. However, when we understand the father's response in the light of the social attitudes of the time, the depth of his love and forgiveness becomes even more apparent. In leaving home and living as he did in the city, this young man had disgraced not only himself but the entire village as well. He had committed grievous sins. According to the Law, the leaders had a right to put him to death. If he had entered the village alone, the people would have stoned him on the spot. Thus, the father's response was one of protection as well as love and forgiveness. In throwing his arms around his son, the father was saying, in effect, "Go ahead. Throw all the stones you want. However, in doing so, you must kill me also."

What a beautiful picture of what Christ has done for us! He suffered and died on the cross, bearing the guilt of all our sins. As a result, when we come to Him, He throws His arms around us and gladly welcomes us home. Sadly, however, many Christians are often unwilling to show this same forgiveness to others. And this unwillingness to forgive is one of the major causes of anger in us.

The elder son was probably also angered by the fact that his father had *favored* his brother. Once the younger son was safely in the house, his father instructed the servants to kill the fatted calf and to prepare a lavish feast in his honor. Normally, a prized calf was used only for a special occasion, such as a wedding or a religious feast. Because of his own unforgiving attitude, the elder brother could not understand why his father would want to celebrate his younger brother's return. After all, he had disgraced the entire family. He certainly didn't deserve to be treated so well. Likewise, the Scriptures indicate that the elder son may have been harboring a secret desire for his father to have a party for him and his friends (see Luke 15:29). Thus, the elder brother became jealous of the attention and rewards that his brother was receiving, and he became angry at his father for giving them to him.

Unfortunately, many Christians have this same attitude toward their Heavenly Father. We hold grudges against God and become angry at Him whenever He appears to favor another believer over us. I've met pastors who were angry at God because some fellow pastor had a larger and more productive church than he had. I've met Sunday school teachers who were holding a grudge against God because another class had received privileges their class had not been given. I've met believers who were angry at God because their children were rebelling or because they couldn't have children or for some other reason. This attitude, probably more than any other, is a source of dissension and division in the church.

A lack of forgiveness and jealousy on his part led the elder brother to become angry at his father for loving and forgiving his brother. Likewise, *he became angry at his brother* for these and other reasons. Behind the elder brother's anger was *fear*. He feared his brother's return because his own weakness would then be exposed. The fact that his younger brother had deserted his father and was living in sin made the older brother look that much better. No doubt, the people had been praising the older son for his faithfulness to his father. And the elder brother liked his new position of honor. If his brother returned and began to make up for his past sins and failures, he would lose much of his prestige.

Notice that when the younger son returned, his older brother was not even aware of it until he heard the celebration taking place. Why? Because he had not been looking for his return. He didn't believe that his younger brother would ever repent and come home again, nor did he want him to. When he was in the fields, he had not shielded his eyes and looked up, hoping to see his brother. His father, on the other hand, had often scanned the horizon for signs of his son. Thus, when the son did return, his father spotted him when he was still a long way off (see Luke 15:20).

What is your reaction to believers who have sinned and turned away from the Lord? Do you grieve over them, pray for them and try to help them return to the Lord? Are you willing to welcome them again into the fellowship when they repent? Or do you write them off, saying, "If they want to live that way, let them. I hope I never see them again"?

In addition, the elder brother was angry at his brother because he feared the competition. His brother's return was a threat to him. When he saw his father giving his brother so much, he was afraid that he would not receive all he hoped to get. After all, he reasoned, his brother had already been given his inheritance and had squandered it. Thus, his father was giving his brother what rightfully belonged to him. When he angrily confronted his father about the matter, he was told, "Son, thou art ever with me, and all that I have is thine" (v. 30). The father's love for the elder son had not changed. That son's position in the family and his inheritance would always remain the same.

The same is true of God's love for us. We need to remember that there is no competition in the family of God. Our Heavenly Father loves all of His children equally. When another child enters the family,

His love and kindness are never divided—only multiplied. First John 4:18-21 emphatically states, "There is no fear in love; but perfect [mature] love casteth out fear: because fear hath torment. He that feareth is not made perfect in love. We love him, because he first loved us. If a man say, I love God, and hateth his brother, he is a liar: for he that loveth not his brother whom he hath seen, how can he love God whom he hath not seen? And this commandment have we from him, That he who loveth God love his brother also."

When we fail to understand how much God loves us, fear and anger soon take over. And we find we are unable to love others as we should. Because the elder brother did not love his father and his brother as he should have, he harbored anger and resentment toward them. His hostility was evident.

Less apparent, but probably even more important, was the fact that *he was angry at himself.* Why would he be angry at himself? The answer to this question lies in his motives for staying home and serving his father. The elder son's service was not motivated by a deep love for his father and a desire to serve him. He was mainly concerned about what he could get for himself. When he did not receive the rewards he felt he deserved, he inwardly became more rebellious and dissatisfied. Thus, while he did not physically leave home, his mind, heart and will had deserted his father long before his brother left. He spent his life plotting how to get what he wanted from his father. And when his agenda did not work out as he had planned, he was angry at himself for conforming outwardly to what was expected.

What this man did not realize was that his father would have given him what he wanted if he had only asked for it. If he had said, "You know, Dad, I've been working hard lately. I could really use some time off. Would you mind if I killed the fatted calf and invited some of my friends over for a party?" his father would have gladly agreed to his request. But, instead of asking, he allowed resentment and anger toward his father—and himself—to build up. This, in turn, caused him to become self-righteous. Thus, when he saw his father rewarding his younger brother, he retorted indignantly, "All these years I have faithfully served you. Not once have I disobeyed your orders. Yet you have never even given me so much as a young goat so I could have a party with my friends. But my disobedient, rebellious brother comes home, and what do you do? You immediately kill the best calf we have and throw a big celebration for him. It's just not fair!" (see Luke 15:29,30).

We can just imagine this man standing outside the house and pouting while the party is going on inside. When his father comes out and begs him to join them, the elder brother throws a huge temper tantrum. The elder son's childishness is revealed in the way that his father responded. His father treated him like a small child, gently scolding, "Son, thou art ever with me" (v. 31). The Greek word translated "son" in this passage means "child." It is not the word for a mature son. The father was

143

saying, in effect, "You're being immature. Please stop acting like a child and welcome your brother home."

While the elder son was doing his father's work, he was not doing his father's will. His obedience did not come from his heart (see Eph. 6:6). He was only concerned about appearing righteous in the eyes of others. He pretended to serve his father, when he was really serving himself. He was like the Pharisees of Jesus' day. No doubt their pride and self-righteousness were deeply wounded by this parable.

But what about us? Don't we often do the same thing? We need to examine our own motives for service. Are we serving out of a deep love for our Lord and for others, or do we love ourselves too much? Do we serve only to receive praise and recognition from others? If so, then we will likely respond in anger when others are blessed or honored more than we are.

What Did It Cost Him?

The price of nurturing anger is high indeed! The elder brother paid dearly for his anger. What did it cost him to remain outside? First, we see that *he lost his fellowship with his father.* He turned his father into an employer, working for gain instead of love. Thus, he missed many of the benefits that were his because of his position as a son.

Because the elder son's fellowship was gone, *he lost his joy.* His work became a burden instead of a blessing. As a result, *he lost his love* for his brother—and for his father. His jealousy and resentment over his brother's leaving caused him to reject his brother when he returned. He refused even to talk with him, much less forgive him and welcome him back. This, in turn, caused him to blame his father and to cut himself off from his love. The same thing is true in the Christian life. We cannot separate our love for God from our love for others. The two must go together. God has made it clear in His Word that when we reject other believers, we reject Him as well (see I John 4:19-21).

In addition, the elder son lost one of his most valuable possessions, for *he lost his character.* Phillips Brooks said that the purpose of life is the building of character through truth. God's Word is truth. And God is in the process of building sons and daughters that He can be proud of. When we look closely at the parable of the Prodigal Son, we discover that the younger son had a more admirable character in some respects. Even though he had disgraced his father's name, he showed great courage and humility when he was willing to say, "Father, please forgive me for hurting you so terribly. I know I am not worthy to be called your son. However, I want to do your will. So make me one of your servants" (see Luke 15:18,19). The older son, on the other hand, outwardly was obedient while inwardly he remained rebellious.

In looking at the contrast between these two men—and their father's response—we discover the Lord's attitude toward sin in our lives. While the Prodigal Son was guilty of the sins of the flesh, his brother was guilty of the sins of the spirit. Even

145

though he had not wasted his life in riotous living, the older son had used precious time and energy on unrighteous anger. The elder brother would not have gone to the far country, but he had the far country in his heart. In this parable, and throughout the New Testament, we find Jesus placing more emphasis on our attitudes than on our actions. Outward obedience is worthless in God's eyes if our heart is not right with Him.

Because the elder brother had lost his love and his joy, *he lost his opportunity to help other people.* When the younger son returned home, his father held a feast in his honor. No doubt many of their friends and neighbors were there. They knew that the elder brother had refused to come to the celebration. Perhaps some of them looked out the window and witnessed the angry scene between him and his father. They were probably saying to themselves, *My, how we have misjudged that boy. Here we thought he was such a good son. But he is just as disobedient as his younger brother.* Any chance that the elder brother would have had to tell these people about the grace and mercy of God was lost because of his pride and anger.

Nothing is more devastating than the bad example of a good man. When the unsaved sin, no one thinks twice about it. However, when a believer falls, it affects not only his testimony but the testimony of fellow believers as well. And no sin is more obvious to others than anger. When we harbor anger toward God, toward others and toward ourselves, it will always come out eventually. And anger exacts a heavy toll on our character, on our opportunities for service and on our love for others. Are you willing to pay the price for your anger?

How Can He Come Inside?

When we consider the high cost of anger, we can see the urgency of finding ways to deal with it. Unresolved anger seriously harms our relationship with God and with others and keeps us outside the fellowship of believers. Therefore, we must ask ourselves a third—and perhaps the most important—question, "How can we come inside?"

We don't know whether or not the elder brother ever asked himself this question. But if he had, he would have discovered several important steps that he must take in order to enter again. These are the same steps that we must take in order to restore our fellowship with God and with others. First, he had to *see himself honestly*.

At the heart of the elder son's anger was pride. He was too proud to admit his own sin. Likewise, he had an erroneous view of sin. He believed that sin was only external (specific actions) rather than internal (wrong attitudes) as well. However, the Bible makes it clear that two kinds of sin exist. There are sins of the flesh and sins of the spirit. There are sins of disposition and sins of dissipation. The younger son had a problem with the sins of the flesh. He gave in to his desire to enjoy the pleasures of the moment. On the other hand, the older son's problem lay in his character. He had the wrong

147

attitudes, and sinful attitudes are much more difficult to deal with.

Like the elder brother, most of us would not think of committing the sins that the Prodigal Son did. However, what about our attitudes? Have we been guilty of criticism, gossip or backbiting? When the elder brother was confronted with his own sin, he immediately dragged up the past sins of his brother, replying, "This thy son was come, which hath devoured thy living with harlots" (Luke 15:30). Unfortunately, some people are so busy hanging out other people's dirty laundry in public that they don't have time to clean up their own lives.

The scribes and Pharisees were often guilty of this same self-righteous attitude. They were so busy pointing out the sins of others that they never really saw themselves as God did. In the parable of the Pharisee and the publican, Jesus clearly condemned their sinful attitudes (see 18:9-14).

Instead of pointing out the sins of his brother, the elder son should have been looking closely at his own life and honestly admitting his guilt. Then he needed to *yield to the father and confess his sins*. However, the Scriptures do not indicate that he ever did this. While the younger brother said, "I have sinned against heaven, and in thy sight" (15:21), we don't find the elder brother saying, "I have sinned." Before we can rid our hearts of the poison of anger, we must yield to the Father.

Likewise, the elder brother also needed to *be reconciled to his brother*. While the Scriptures do not specifically say this, it is likely that the two brothers were not getting along even before the younger brother left home.

Reconciliation is extremely important. So often we think that once we come privately to God and confess our sins, the problem is settled. However, Jesus has told us that before we come to His altar, we must first go and be reconciled with our brother (see Matt. 5:21-24). I can recall times in my life when I've had to go to a brother or sister in Christ and say, "I'm sorry. I've sinned against you. My attitude was wrong, and I want you to forgive me."

Finally, before the elder brother could enter the joyful fellowship, he needed to *be thankful.* Even after the elder brother admitted his guilt, confessed his sin to his father and brother and was reconciled to them, he still would have remained on the outside looking in unless he was truly thankful for his brother's return.

Anger locks the door of our heart and keeps us from enjoying true fellowship with God and with our brothers and sisters in Christ. What will open the door? Surrender and joy. We must willingly surrender our lives to the Lord, giving Him our anger and other sinful attitudes. Once we do, we will know true joy. And with His joy in our hearts, there will be no room for anger.

Chapter 12

The Anger of Jesus

Many people have the mistaken idea that Christians should get along with everyone, that we should never become angry at others. But, as we have seen, the Scriptures clearly indicate that some forms of anger are not only justified—they are commanded. Those who condemn all forms of anger frequently point to Jesus as their example. However, you don't have to read very far in the Gospels before you discover that Jesus did not get along with everyone. He even became angry with people on several occasions. In fact, Christ aroused the anger of the crowd so much that they eventually crucified Him.

Of course, Jesus is remembered most for His compassion for the fallen, the lost, the afflicted, the sorrowing, the helpless. And indeed He is a compassionate and loving God. However, we should not forget His courage and His holy anger. Because God is light, as well as love, He must express a holy indignation and anger toward sin. To do otherwise would deny His holiness and His love. Pure and righteous anger is not a sign of sin but of love. Conviction without love leads to bigotry. Love without conviction is only sentimentality. But love

150

plus conviction equals ministry. And this is what Jesus Christ displayed when He was here on earth.

Because Jesus loves us so much, He cannot tolerate evil in our lives. We should have this same attitude: "Ye that love the Lord, hate evil" (Ps. 97:10). And standing up for what is right frequently causes us to have enemies. Jesus did not get along with everyone. At times He had to express holy anger against sin in the lives of people. He has set the example for us to follow in displaying our anger. He shows us the only reason for becoming angry— sin. He shows us how to express that anger in constructive ways. Let's examine several incidents in the life of Christ to discover what sins in particular aroused His holy anger.

Hardness of Heart

When we look at the life and ministry of Jesus, we see Him expressing anger again and again at three different sins. The first sin that especially aroused His anger was the hardness of people's hearts. In Mark 3:1-7 we read: "And he entered again into the synagogue; and there was a man there which had a withered hand. And they watched him, whether he would heal him on the sabbath day; that they might accuse him. And he saith unto the man which had the withered hand, Stand forth. And he saith unto them, Is it lawful to do good on the sabbath days, or to do evil? to save life, or to kill? But they held their peace. And when he had looked round about on them with anger, being grieved for the hardness of their hearts, he saith unto the man, Stretch forth thine hand. And he stretched it out: and his hand was restored whole as the other. And the Pharisees went forth, and straightway took counsel with the Herodians against him, how they might destroy him. But Jesus withdrew himself with his disciples to the sea."

Jesus saw the Pharisees' hardness of heart (see Luke 6:7), and it deeply grieved and angered Him. The word translated "hardness" in Mark 3:5 is more accurately rendered "hardening." The process of hardening was occurring at that time, and it grieved the Lord. Notice where they were. They were in the synagogue on the Sabbath. Like the ruler we looked at in Chapter 10, these scribes and Pharisees had respect for Jewish tradition but no concern for a needy man. They were only using him as bait in their attempt to trap the Lord Jesus. Christ, on the other hand, saw this handicapped man as a person made in the image of God. He felt compassion for him and healed him. Nothing is more tragic than when we treat people as a means to an end and not as an end in themselves.

In this incident we see that the Pharisees' motive for being in the synagogue that day was wrong. They were not there to worship and to learn. They didn't believe that they needed this teaching. After all, they reasoned, who was more religious than they were? They studied the Scriptures continually and followed the Law to the letter. They prayed and tithed faithfully. They attended the synagogue services every Sabbath.

So why were the scribes and Pharisees in the

synagogue that day? They weren't there to listen to what Jesus had to say. They had already rejected Him. They only came to see what they could find to criticize.

Sadly, many Christians today are guilty of the same attitude. They don't come to church to worship and to learn; they come to criticize and gossip. An incident in the life of Joseph Parker, the great British preacher, illustrates this tragic truth. He was preaching at the City Temple in London. After the service one of the listeners came up to him and said, "Dr. Parker, you made a grammatical error in your sermon." He then proceeded to point out the error to the pastor. Joseph Parker looked at the man and said, "And what else did you get out of the message?" What a perfect rebuke! No one is perfect. Pastors, teachers, soloists, ushers—they all make mistakes. Occasionally, each one of us says or does the wrong thing (see James 3:2). This is natural. However, our reason for going to church is not to be critical of others but to worship the Lord and allow His message to speak to us. We should be concerned only about ourselves and how we can serve the Lord better. A critical spirit has no place in the family of God. It only causes division and dissension.

Because their hearts were hard and unyielding, the scribes and Pharisees had no compassion for the man with the withered hand. They refused to listen to the Word of God. They became critical and vengeful and, as a result, brought God's judgment on themselves.

153

This had always been Israel's problem. Time and time again they had hardened their hearts against God and had refused to obey Him. The Prophet Zechariah knew this all too well: "And the word of the Lord came unto Zechariah, saying, Thus speaketh the Lord of hosts, saying, Execute true judgment, and shew mercy and compassions every man to his brother: and oppress not the widow, nor the fatherless, the stranger, nor the poor; and let none of you imagine evil against his brother in your heart. But they refused to hearken, and pulled away the shoulder, and stopped their ears, that they should not hear. Yea, they made their hearts as an adamant stone, lest they should hear the law, and the words which the Lord of hosts hath sent in his spirit by the former prophets: therefore came a great wrath from the Lord of hosts" (Zech. 7:8-12).

The Lord was tremendously angered and grieved at the Pharisees' rebellious and stubborn attitude. He was angry at the way they treated the man and grieved at the way they were treating themselves and God. Mark 3:5 states, "And when he had looked round about on them with anger." Notice the tense of the verbs in this passage. Christ's anger was not the slow, seething kind of anger that remains and grows. It was a righteous indignation that was quickly aroused and was just as quickly quenched. However, the phrase "being grieved" (v. 5) is a present participle. It indicates a continuous action. Thus, while Jesus was only angry at them for a moment, He constantly grieved over their hardness of heart. The same should be true of

154

our anger. Our anger should be motivated by a deep and constant sense of grief at what sin is doing to others. While we should be angry at the sin, we should feel only sorrow for the sinner.

Jesus Christ is still grieving over the hardness of people's hearts—people who listen to the Word of God just to find something to criticize, people who are not concerned about the needs of others, people who sit in the house of God pretending to be righteous.

Notice how Jesus dealt with His anger and grief. Rather than staying and arguing with the Pharisees, He simply left (see v. 7). He knew that once a person has rejected His truth and hardened his heart against Him, all the arguments in the world will not change his mind. The Lord does not force Himself on us. If we do not want His truth and His salvation, He will go to someone who does. But it grieves Him greatly to have to do this.

Frequently we must deal with our anger in the same way. Often the best solution is simply to walk away from the person with whom we are angry. This is especially true when the person has hardened his heart against us and against the Lord. In most cases, trying to reason with the person does little good. Rather than trying to change him, we should simply forgive him and commit him to the Lord.

Pride

In Mark 10 we discover a second sin that angers the Lord Jesus—pride. He will not tolerate pride

155

because it is born of selfishness. And the only cure for pride is to become like a child: "And they brought young children to him, that he should touch them: and his disciples rebuked those that brought them. But when Jesus saw it, he was much displeased, and said unto them, Suffer the little children to come unto me, and forbid them not: for of such is the kingdom of God. Verily I say unto you, Whosoever shall not receive the kingdom of God as a little child, he shall not enter therein. And he took them up in his arms, put his hands upon them, and blessed them" (vv. 13-16).

What a beautiful scene! In that day, it was customary for parents to bring their children to the rabbis for a blessing. In many places where Jesus stopped, He was met by parents who were hoping to have their children blessed by the Great Teacher. It is interesting to note that the word "those" in verse 13 is masculine. Many people have assumed that the mothers were the only ones who brought children to see Jesus. However, this passage indicates that the fathers also brought the little ones. I thank God for fathers who love the Lord and their children enough to raise their children to know Him. One of the greatest blessings we can receive is to have a father who knows the Lord, who prays and who wants his children to come to Jesus.

We should also note that these parents were not bringing their children to Jesus to be baptized by Him. How do we know this? John 4:2 tells us that Jesus never baptized anyone, although His disciples frequently did. However, considering the disciples' reaction to the children in this incident in Mark 10, it is unlikely that the disciples baptized the children. The disciples were scolding the parents for bothering Jesus.

One of the things that I miss most about my pastoral ministry in a local church is the privilege of dedicating children and parents to the Lord. What a joy to watch parents bring children into the world and then dedicate them to the Lord's service! As I visit my former pastorates, I often meet many of the children that I dedicated. What a joy it is to see that they are serving the Lord now that they are grown.

When the parents brought their children to Jesus to be blessed, the disciples opposed them. Why? Because they were proud and thought they knew best. Thus, instead of seeking the Lord's will in the matter, they tried to handle the situation themselves. And, as they soon discovered, they had much to learn.

Why did the disciples become proud? Because they had wrong views about the Lord and about themselves. First, we see that they had *a wrong view of the Lord's ministry*. At this point in Christ's ministry, the disciples still did not understand His purpose for coming to earth. They believed that Jesus would overthrow the Roman government and set up an earthly kingdom. Thus, they could see no reason for wasting time on children who would be of no use in such a kingdom. But the Lord told them, "Suffer the little children to come unto me, and forbid them not: for of such is the kingdom of

157

God" (Mark 10:14). They were probably still pondering these words when a rich young ruler came to see Jesus (see vv. 17-22). Here was a man who had influence and money. In the disciples' eyes, he was a valuable asset to the Lord's ministry. Yet Jesus treated him like He did anyone else. The disciples were perplexed. They still didn't understand the purpose of Christ's ministry. They couldn't see that Jesus was not concerned about a person's affluence. What mattered was his attitude.

Unfortunately, many Christians today still have this same problem. We still don't understand the kingdom of God. Thus, we give preferential treatment to certain people and ignore others. And often children are ignored the most. I had this vividly illustrated to me as I was preaching in a church one Sunday. As I visited with the pastor between services, a group of children raced past us, laughing and having a good time. The pastor quickly apologized for their behavior, saying, "Brother Wiersbe, I'm sorry for all that commotion." I replied, "Don't apologize. Jesus would love it. After all, He's the One who threw the adults out of the temple and told the children to stay and sing their praises to God."

Because the disciples' view of the Lord's ministry was erroneous, they also had *a wrong view of children.* They thought that children were not important to the Lord Jesus. However, Christ has a high regard and a great love for children. They are precious to Him. He was never too busy to spend time with them or to talk with them. In fact, He compared true believers to children on several occasions. He said, "Those who want to follow Me must become like a little child" (see v. 15). Jesus did not mean that we should be *childish*. He was talking about being *childlike*. A child is humble. He is willing to be dependent on his parents. He is trusting and believes without reservation what he is told. A child is open-minded and eager to learn. He is always looking for the wonder and joy of life. He sees the best in everyone. This is the kind of faith that Christ wants us to have.

I imagine that the Lord is deeply grieved at the way children are treated today. So many children are being abused physically, mentally and emotionally. Scores of others are being ignored and neglected. Even believers have wrong attitudes toward children at times. We do not see them as important. We make no real efforts to lead them to the Lord. When they come to us and express a desire to accept Jesus, we often question whether they are old enough to understand such a commitment. What about you? Are you doing what you can to reach the children of the world for Christ? Jesus says to us, "Permit the little children to come to Me and forbid them not. Don't stand in their way."

At the heart of the disciples' pride was the fact that they had *a wrong view of themselves*. They believed that they had a right to make decisions for the Lord. They thought they knew what was best for the ministry. So they proceeded to do things their own way and to ignore the Lord completely. Their pride and selfishness angered Jesus. In a graphic way He reminded them of the fact that

"God resisteth the proud, but giveth grace unto the humble" (James 4:6).

Hypocrisy

Mark 11 records one of the best-known examples of Christ's anger. In this incident we find a sin that is very grievous to the Lord—hypocrisy. "And they come to Jerusalem: and Jesus went into the temple, and began to cast out them that sold and bought in the temple, and overthrew the tables of the money-changers, and the seats of them that sold doves; and would not suffer that any man should carry any vessel through the temple. And he taught, saying unto them, Is it not written, My house shall be called of all nations the house of prayer? but ye have made it a den of thieves. And the scribes and chief priests heard it, and sought how they might destroy him: for they feared him, because all the people was astonished at his doctrine" (vv. 15-18). Our Lord hates hypocrisy.

When God gave the Law to the Children of Israel, He also gave them detailed instructions of how He wanted them to worship Him. The Lord instituted the practice of animal sacrifice in order to prepare the people for the coming of the Messiah. But, as they did with many of God's laws, the Israelites added stipulations and rules to the law concerning sacrifices. By the time of Christ, the Pharisees had turned the sacrifices into big business. They required the people to purchase the animals from vendors at the temple—at greatly inflated prices.

The Jewish leaders were using the worship services for their own gain.

This was the situation that Jesus faced. As He entered the temple that day, He didn't see a house of worship. He saw a religious supermarket. No wonder He was angry! The people had turned His holy institution into a racket. He told them, "You have turned My house into a den of thieves" (see v. 17). Jesus was reminding them of God's words to them in Jeremiah 7:11: "Is this house, which is called by my name, become a den of robbers in your eyes? Behold, even I have seen it, saith the Lord." What is a den of robbers? It's the place where thieves run to hide after they have committed a crime. Thus, Jesus was strongly condemning the people for their hypocrisy. They were pretending to worship God when, in reality, they were only using the temple as a place to hide their sins.

Using the Lord's house as a place of business was bad enough if only the Jews had been involved. But they were presenting a bad testimony to the Gentiles as well. Why? Because they were conducting their business in the Court of the Gentiles. This was the only area in the entire temple where the Gentiles could go to worship God. The Jews should have been there trying to lead the Gentiles to the Lord by showing them the glory of God and by opening His Word to them. But they were cheating them instead.

I wonder what the Lord would do today if He entered some of our churches and religious organizations? So many people today are using the name

161

of Christ to gain power, money and influence. Their bad testimony is causing the unsaved to turn away from the truth of God. I'm sure God's greatest judgment is reserved for these religious racketeers—people who pose as holy and spiritual while they use their position and opportunities for personal gain.

When is anger holy and constructive? When it is displayed according to the example of Jesus. While the Lord hates all sin, He is especially angry at the sins of the heart. He is angered and grieved when people's hearts become so hard that they are unable to feel love and compassion for others. He hates a critical spirit. He is angered by selfish pride that causes us to hinder those who want to come to Him. And, most of all, Jesus hates hypocrisy. He is angered by people who pretend to be spiritual, who turn religion into a racket and then try to cover it up with prayers and songs.

Hardness of heart, pride, hypocrisy—these are not the sins only of the unsaved but also of Christians. The Lord will not tolerate deception in His children, and neither should we. We should be angered and grieved when we see these sins in our church, our fellow believers—and ourselves. This righteous anger should cause us to speak out against such sin and to seek to lead the sinners back to the Lord. When anger is displayed with love, humility and self-control, the Lord will use it for our good and His glory.

Back to the Bible is a nonprofit ministry dedicated to Bible teaching, evangelism and edification of Christians worldwide.

If we may assist you in knowing more about Christ and the Christian life, please write to us without obligation:

Back to the Bible
P.O. Box 82808
Lincoln, NE 68501